MASTERING

*personal finance*

## Palgrave Master Series

Accounting
Accounting Skills
Advanced English Language
Advanced Pure Mathematics
Arabic
Basic Management
Biology
British Politics
Business Communication
Business Environment
C Programming
C++ Programming
Chemistry
COBOL Programming
Communication
Computing
Counselling Skills
Counselling Theory
Customer Relations
Database Design
Delphi Programming
Desktop Publishing
e-Business
Economic and Social History
Economics
Electrical Engineering
Electronics
Employee Development
English Grammar
English Language
English Literature
Fashion Buying and Merchandising
  Management
Fashion Marketing
Fashion Styling
Financial Management
Geography
Global Information Systems
Globalization of Business
Human Resource Management

Information Technology
International Trade
Internet
Java
Language of Literature
Management Skills
Marketing Management
Mathematics
Microsoft Office
Microsoft Windows, Novell
  NetWare and UNIX
Modern British History
Modern European History
Modern German History
Modern United States History
Modern World History
Networks
Novels of Jane Austen
Organisational Behaviour
Pascal and Delphi Programming
Personal Finance
Philosophy
Physics
Poetry
Practical Criticism
Psychology
Public Relations
Shakespeare
Social Welfare
Sociology
Spanish
Statistics
Strategic Management
Systems Analysis and Design
Team Leadership
Theology
Twentieth-Century Russian History
Visual Basic
World Religions

www.palgravemasterseries.com

**Macmillan Master Series**
Series Standing Order ISBN 0-333-69343-4
(outside North America only)

You can receive future titles in this series as they are published by
placing a standing order. Please contact your bookseller or, in case
of difficulty, write to us at the address below with your name and
address, the title of the series and the ISBN quoted above.

Customer Services Department, Macmillan Distribution Ltd
Houndmills, Basingstoke, Hampshire RG21 6XS, England

# MASTERING

## personal finance

John Gorham

palgrave
macmillan

First published 2008 by
PALGRAVE MACMILLAN
Houndmills, Basingstoke, Hampshire RG21 6XS and
175 Fifth Avenue, New York, N.Y. 10010
Companies and representatives throughout the world

PALGRAVE MACMILLAN is the global academic imprint of the
Palgrave Macmillan division of St. Martin's Press, LLC and of Palgrave
Publishers Ltd. Macmillan® is a registered trademark in the United
States, United Kingdom and other countries. Palgrave is a registered
trademark in the European Union and other countries.

ISBN-13: 978-0-230-55301-9
ISBN-10: 0-230-55301-X

The book is printed on paper suitable for recycling and made
from fully managed and sustained forest sources. Logging, pulping
and manufacturing processes are expected to conform to the
environmental regulations of the country of origin.

A catalogue record for this book is available from the British Library.

10   9   8   7   6   5   4   3   2   1
17   16   15   14   13   12   11   10   09   08

Printed and bound in Great Britain by
Creative Print & Design (Wales), Ebbw Vale

This book is intended as a general introduction to personal finance
and not as a basis for advice to specific individuals. easonable steps
have been taken to ensure the facts as they are stated in the book
are correct but they are subject to change. Neither the author or the
publisher can take responsibility for any loss or problem arising from
any of the information provided within and you should consult a
suitably qualified person for specific advice.

To the memory of my parents

Contents

# a note from the author

I am starting to write this preface at Christmas-time 2006. The book itself is nearly complete. Even so, I am conscious that there is more to do and I have a deadline only a few weeks away.

As tends to happen at Christmas, my mind keeps wandering back to when I was a lad. Christmas is still special but it does not arouse the same excitement that it did 50 years ago.

Life generally was very different in 1956. The Second World War had ended only eleven years before and I had arrived in this world eight days after VE Day. Rationing had lasted a few more years but by 1956 I was familiar with the joys of chocolate, fizzy drinks, pineapple chunks and other "unhealthy" goodies.

I had some lovely toys by the standards of the day. I revelled in Minibricks, Meccano, Airfix kits and Dinky Toys but my real passion was model trains. My younger brother Martin shared that passion and we were of course still in the era of steam.

The year 1956 was significant in many ways. I sat the eleven-plus examination at the start of the year and subsequently made the transition from junior to senior school. There was a family gathering in Suffolk at which I collected 38 autographs and, a couple of weeks later, Dad, Mum, Martin and I had a guided tour round the *Queen Mary* – the three-funnel version used as a troop ship in the Second World War – in Southampton Dock.

For a giddy eleven-year-old, however, Christmas was the high spot. I was promised in September an electric train set and the three and a half months' wait to 25 December was sheer agony. Part of the cost had to come out of my pocket money but the day finally arrived and I was not disappointed.

I do not recall thinking much about money in those days – it was in short supply. Dad was a headmaster so we were comfortably off compared with many families. Even so, money was often tight and much of what Martin and I enjoyed was down to Mum's shrewd financial skills. She too had been a teacher and, like Dad, was a strict disciplinarian. Woe betide Martin or me if we stepped out of line – or, more accurately, if we were discovered doing so.

On my starting at grammar school in September 1956, Dad announced an increase in my pocket money from a shilling (5 new pence) a week to half a crown (12½ new pence). I felt like a millionaire; I had never enjoyed such riches before.

The announcement was accompanied by a lecture on how to manage my new-found wealth. I can still picture the scene in my mind's eye. Dad and I were sitting in the kitchen as he delivered his briefing in firm but kindly tones. It was my first "formal" lesson in personal finance and one that probably made more impact than a career of 36½ years in banking.

I drifted into banking in 1965 and specialised immediately in executor and trustee work. My five years with Glyn, Mills & Co. had a lasting and profound impact; it was a sad day in 1970 when, inevitably, "Glyns" was absorbed into a larger organisation. I had had all sorts of experiences including a stint in general banking during which I was taught to lend money – but I hate being in debt myself. I was even seconded to a stockbroker for a couple of months to learn about investment and saw a side to life that I had never imagined.

I reached the rank of bank manager at a relatively tender age. I never became, however, "a nice old bank manager" in the mould of Captain Mainwaring of BBC Television's "Dad's Army"; my forte was as a "technocrat" rather than one versed in diplomatic skills (not that Captain Mainwaring was any better). When regulation hit the financial services industry in the mid-1980s, I soon found myself poring through regulations and writing compliance manuals as part of a shift in culture.

Personal finance has grown as an interest both professionally and from a personal point of view. In addition, my mother was a widow for nearly fifteen years and dealing with the challenges of her advancing years – practical and financial – added a dimension to my experience. My own retirement has encouraged me to look at issues in different ways and to make comparisons with how things were done in my day.

Perhaps I can offer some perceptions of the pressing financial issues of today and comparisons with my experiences during the last forty years or so.

Firstly, there is the attitude to – and tolerance of – personal debt and the relative ease with which people can borrow money. Some lenders seem willing to throw money at you, presumably under the pressure of internal business targets.

The financial services industry was far less accessible to "ordinary people" in the 1950s and 1960s than it is today. The providers were more conservative in their outlook and there were clearer demarcations between banks, building societies, brokers, investment managers, lawyers, accountants, and so forth.

Banks, for instance, provided short-term finance and did not lend long-term for house purchase as a matter of course. If you wanted a mortgage, you generally went on your knees to a building society and it helped to have saved with it.

Consumer finance such as hire purchase was not entirely respectable and credit cards had still to appear. The banks provided short-term finance by overdraft, usually against some form of security.

Returning to the present, debt issues are not confined to the UK and one also reads reports of consumer exuberance in the USA especially. Is this healthy for social and moral reasons as well as economic ones? What will happen if and when consumers have a collective change of heart – to their nations and to those that have fed their habit?

Secondly, house prices have been rising relentlessly for several years and, again, it is part of an international trend. An overheated housing market in the USA is worrying economists who are hoping for a soft landing for its economy. Historically low interest rates have no doubt contributed as cheap money has chased after a relatively inelastic supply of houses. The spiral is creating the potential for social imbalances as well as financial ones.

My wife and I bought our house in late 1974 when, mercifully for us, prices had fallen back after the boom of the late 1960s and early 1970s. It was a time of rampant inflation and sky-high interest rates. The price of our house was three to four times my salary and I found the figures daunting. If we were to buy the house now, the multiple would be more like six to eight times an equivalent salary. A hike in interest rates of 1 per cent in 1974 was hardly here or there; it would represent today an increase in the interest rate of 20% for many borrowers.

Thirdly, I have great faith in the financial services industry but is the customer always king? Life assurance is often said to be sold rather than bought and the "endowments mis-selling saga" of recent times lends credence to the saying. I took out a "low-cost" endowment in 1974 to cover my mortgage and received accurate and thorough advice on the options open to me. When the policy matured on my sixtieth birthday, there was no question of a shortfall but a handsome profit instead. Admittedly the growth had fallen back in the last few years but I was content with the outcome.

With-profits endowment policies have served numerous people well over many decades and, in my opinion, the episode in question reflects badly on the industry. A fundamentally sound product has had its reputation tarnished unjustly and what has been the impact on the public's attitude towards long-term savings plans in general?

Fourthly, why is there so much soul-searching over payment for pensions whether through the state or private schemes? Is it not obvious that the cupboard will be bare if we do not set aside enough for the future? I quote later in the book several extracts from the First Report of the Pensions Commission that laid the nation's dilemmas over pensions and savings firmly on the line (see Section 11.6 and Appendix E). "You cannot have your cake and eat it" is surely as valid now as it ever was.

Fifthly, I am disappointed at the level of financial education offered to young people although there are positive signs that the government and others are addressing the problem. Personal finance was less complicated half a century ago when wealth and wealth management services were largely the preserve of an elite. Providers still thought in terms of service, while products were the outputs of manufacturing industry.

I welcome in principle the developments in financial services since my induction in 1965. As with most things, however, some of the 'progress' has been good and some less so. Above all, it is good that consumers should have a wide choice of products and services capable of meeting their needs. A snag is the daunting range on offer and the onerous task of teasing out what is best for you. There is value for the asking if you know what you want and where to find it.

The educational side is the motivation for this book. Industry regulation is now firmly entrenched but an effective regulator is a consumer armed with a sound knowledge of basics and an ability to ask penetrating questions. My primary aim is to nurture those attributes. If people read the book and tell me they have picked up something useful, it will justify the effort.

Finally, I must say something about toys – in a light-hearted vein. I have never experienced a Play station and the sex appeal is lost on me, from a distance at least. I do not understand how they work, how you take them to bits and how you put them together again. What fun is there in pressing buttons all day? How can you be creative and adapt them to your way of thinking?

I still have the train set that so stirred my emotions in 1956. I got it out again some years ago and, after I had unwrapped it from 24-year-old newspapers, the engine worked as well as it had on that magical Christmas Day.

The manufacturer of the train set was Hornby and, as followers of the stock market will know, the company is still thriving and churning out models with features undreamed of in the 1950s. I miss at times playing with my model trains. I miss even more not having bought Hornby shares a few years ago!

# acknowledgements

A number of people have supported me in various ways in the writing of this book and I wish to acknowledge their contributions and thank them accordingly.

Personal finance is a diverse subject and I am convinced of a need for more education and training, particularly for young people. Several people have reinforced the point and I am especially grateful to my cousin Sheila Turner and her husband Dr Eric Turner for their encouragement. They are much closer to the "coal face" of education than I am and have fed me a lot of useful information. In addition, Eric was kind enough to read through my original draft and offer helpful comments on content and style.

My friend and former colleague Peter Ebden and his son John also read through the original draft and I thank them for their constructive remarks. Their differing perspectives, Peter's as a professional and John's as a potential reader, illustrated the challenges of communicating the subject effectively.

My friend Ken Cholerton helped me develop parts of the material on investment. A conversation on investing in emotions (now the subject of Section 9.4) was fascinating and I am grateful for the benefit of his expertise.

Dr James Mallon of the Napier University Business School, Edinburgh reviewed the draft for Palgrave Macmillan and made invaluable suggestions as a teacher and an author of the subject. As a result, I restructured and expanded some of the material and added Chapter 13. I thank him for his contributions.

Others have encouraged me to have a go at writing something, whether on personal finance or a more enjoyable topic such as walking (enjoyment depends of course on one's point of view). My sister-in-law Sylvia Gardner and her husband Peter have taken a keen interest that I value highly.

Personal finance generates as little enthusiasm in my wife Margaret as gardening and fine art conjure up in me. She has, nonetheless, played a key role in terms of encouragement and discipline and I thank her for reading through numerous drafts for sense and meaning. She had a nice way of coming up with the 'blooming obvious' that betrayed a sound grasp of principles!

I have tried hard to ensure accuracy and balance but, if any gremlins have crept in, they are my responsibility and not that of the people who have helped me.

# abbreviations

| | |
|---|---|
| AER | annual equivalent rate |
| AIM | Alternative Investment Market |
| APR | annual percentage rate |
| ATM | automatic teller machine |
| CGT | Capital Gains Tax |
| CT | Corporation Tax |
| CTF | Child Trust Fund |
| DWP | Department of Work and Pensions |
| EIS | enterprise investment scheme |
| EPA | enduring power of attorney |
| ETF | exchange-traded fund |
| FSA | Financial Services Authority |
| FT | *Financial Times* |
| FTSE | *Financial Times* Stock Exchange |
| GDP | gross domestic product |
| GRY | gross redemption yield |
| HIP | Home Information Pack |
| HMRC | Her Majesty's Revenue and Customs |
| IHT | Inheritance Tax |
| ISA | individual savings account |
| IVA | individual voluntary arrangement |
| LPA | lasting power of attorney |
| MPPI | mortgage-payment protection insurance |
| NHS | National Health Service |
| NICs | National Insurance Contributions |
| NS&I | National Savings and Investments |
| OEIC | open-ended investment company |
| PAYE | pay-as-you-earn |
| P/E ratio | price/earnings ratio |
| PEP | personal equity plan |
| pfeg | Personal Finance Education Group |

| | |
|---|---|
| PGO | Public Guardianship Office |
| PIF | property investment fund |
| PIN | personal identity number |
| PMI | private medical insurance |
| PSHE | Personal, Social and Health Education |
| QCA | Qualifications and Curriculum Authority |
| REIT | real-estate investment trust |
| RNCC | registered nursing care contribution |
| RPI | retail prices index |
| S2P | state second pension |
| SDLT | Stamp Duty Land Tax |
| SDRT | Stamp Duty Reserve Tax |
| SIPP | self-invested personal pension |
| SVR | standard variable rate |
| TER | total expense ratio |
| TESSA | tax-exempt special savings account |
| VAT | value added tax |
| VCT | venture capital trust |

# master of your destiny

Introduction – Competence in personal finance – having a sense of purpose

## 1.1 introduction

Personal finance is a big subject and you can get an idea of my interpretation of its scope by glancing down the list of contents. You might think some of the chapters stray beyond the strict realms of personal finance but it is difficult to understand the subject if you do not take account of legal and other frameworks. It is particularly true of Taxation (Chapter 7), Wills and Trusts (Chapter 10) and Buying a home (Chapter 12).

My aim is to help you formulate an approach to matters of personal finance. There is often no right or wrong answer but you are faced with a judgement over options that are better or worse in the particular circumstances.

My fundamental premise is that you need to be master of your own destiny. Ideally, you should have a broad knowledge of the subject and be equipped to research specific themes when they are of interest, or potential interest, to you. You should also be conscious of what might go wrong with a proposed course of action or of doing nothing at all. There are three limbs to the premise.

Firstly, view the 'big picture'. This is a broad-brush or high-level view of what you want to achieve in the management of your personal finances and how you should set about it. The picture also involves an awareness of the industry of personal financial services and what it might offer you in the fulfilment of your aims.

Secondly, study the 'little pictures'. The 'big picture' is conceptual and strategic. By contrast, the 'little pictures' relate to specific issues that warrant a more detailed examination of how they affect you now or in the near future and what products and services are available to meet your needs.

Thirdly, be mindful of what might go wrong, i.e. the risk of losses or hazards. Risk may be inherent in things we choose to do and in events beyond our control. There are often several routes up a mountain, some of which may be more risky than others. Some people are more tolerant of risk than others so that a particular course of action may be better for some and worse for others. The identification of risk and how to tackle it underlies much of the book.

In working through all this, I have in the back of my mind students, mainly young people in their late teens and early twenties. I was one longer ago than I care to remember and I am aware that early twenty-first-century students face pressures that largely passed me by. The system of grants meant that student debt was less of a worry in the 1960s and I was well into my 20s before I faced a salesman who was more concerned with his commission than my interests.

At the same time, personal finance is a great turn-off or mystery for many mature adults. If the book is of any use to them, it will be a bonus for me.

Achieving success in anything involves, among other things, combining competence with a sense of purpose. The next section explores competence in personal finance and the following one looks at having a sense of purpose.

## 1.2 competence in personal finance

Competence in managing one's finances involves, in my opinion, a combination of knowledge and skill. Competence can be innate or acquired by education. What is easy for some is hard for others. I have come across many people who are completely put off by the mention of personal finance even though they are accomplished in other disciplines. The subject, like most others, has its complexities but a lot of it is down to common sense.

### knowledge and skill

Let me return briefly to knowledge and skill. By knowledge I mean having specific information about a subject. Thus you learn what is meant by a mortgage or the attributes of stocks and shares. There are various ways in which you can gain knowledge: reading suitable books, newspapers and journals are obvious examples while the Internet is becoming an excellent source of information. One of my tasks is to lay a foundation on which you can self-build by sensible use of the resources available to you. I refer you also to Section 15.6 and Further reading and resources.

Skill is proficiency acquired by training, in other words instruction and practice. Skill is more about technique than raw knowledge although knowledge is required in the application of the skill. Training may involve tuition by others or self-development.

Professional examinations in financial subjects often reflect the distinction between knowledge and skill. Some of the questions are simply tests of theory. Others are directed to applying the syllabus to situations that might be encountered in real life.

There are an increasing number of complaints in the media about the dearth of formal education in personal finance although, to be fair, initiatives are being taken. Personal finance figures in the National Curriculum as part of Personal, Social and Health Education (PSHE) but is not compulsory. The Qualifications and Curriculum Authority (QCA) is developing a new subject called Functional Maths for introduction in England in 2008 to help teach pupils the basics of looking after money; it is expected to feature in the GCSE mathematics syllabuses from 2008.

HM Treasury published a document on the Government's long-term approach to 'Financial Capability' on 15 January 2007 in response to concerns over low levels of financial awareness across the UK. The report set out, among other things, aspirations in relation to adults having access to general financial advice and to educational programmes for all children and young people (see www.hm-treasury.gov.uk).[1]

The private sector is also taking an interest. In early 2006, the *ifs* School of Finance announced personal-finance qualifications for general release to schools. Financial services businesses are also supporters of the Personal Finance Education Group (pfeg), an educational charity directed to teaching young people, the skills and knowledge they need in financial matters.

One of the roles of parents is to help equip their offspring with life skills. I regard managing one's finances as a key skill but I doubt that everyone agrees. In any event, personal finance is a vast subject and even the professionals tend to focus on particular aspects. It is down to individuals to decide what is right for them.

My concern is with people who are keen to learn but are bemused over how to set about it. I am encouraging you to become master of your own destiny and I now seek to justify it. My most compelling reason is rooted in the difficulties of relying on someone else to do things for you.

Whoever you might engage, you still need to set the direction and make key decisions; you cannot opt out completely. There are precious few advisers who are fully conversant in all relevant areas of expertise and, if you found such a paragon, the costs would be considerable if not prohibitive. Even then, how can you be sure that your best interests are being placed before those of your agent?

Most people need to take professional advice at some time or other and it is prudent and cost-effective to do so. On the other hand, a lot of personal finance boils down to common sense and having a working knowledge is an effective defence whether you are dealing direct with a supplier or seeking the help of an agent. You should at least know the sort of things to look out for and be primed to ask the right questions.

In Section 1.1, I attached three limbs to my fundamental premise of mastering your destiny: the 'big picture' and the 'little pictures' coupled with a consideration of what might go wrong. You rarely start with a blank sheet but, for those who can, I recommend gaining a familarity with the 'big picture' before drilling deeper into the 'little pictures' of specific topics.

The purpose of this book is to paint a 'big picture'. It involves some preliminary sketches of the 'little pictures' and an attempt to work them into a meaningful

---

1 The Children, Schools and Families Secretary announced on 12 July 2007 significant revisions to the National Curriculum for secondary schools. From September 2008, it would have room for a new subject, 'Economic well-being and financial capability', that would incorporate topics on personal finance.

landscape. Hence, in Chapter 14, I work through a case study that is based on the outline biography in Section 1.3 below.

The management of risk is a recurrent theme and is part of developing a healthy attitude to personal finance. One has to accept the need to take risks and to manage them by learning to evaluate objectively whether a risk is worth taking or not.

## coping with risk

The starting point is to ask yourself what can go wrong?. It is easy to get carried away by the emotion of the moment and to lose sight of the realities of tomorrow.

The evaluation of risk sounds grandiose but it need not be so in practice. One can take specific steps such as buying insurance against an identifiable contingency or adopting generic behaviours like setting money aside for a rainy day and living comfortably within one's income. Evaluation leads to the equation of whether or not the rewards of taking the risk outweigh the potential harm of things going wrong plus the cost of covering your back.

In other words, recognise the risks, evaluate them, do what you can to mitigate them and accept the rest. If things still turn out badly, you can at least say that you tried and hope for better luck next time.

I devote Chapter 5 to borrowing and it can be a much riskier affair than it might seem at first sight. My parents used to come out with all sorts of little quips and sayings some of which were amusing and others which were wise. To my shame, I have forgotten many but 'neither a borrower nor lender be' (Shakespeare; Hamlet, I, iii) has stuck through thick and thin.

Borrowing and lending help make the world go round and have done so since time immemorial. I am not suggesting, however, that my parents' advice was totally flawed. It is a question of how one interprets the principle lying behind it.

Relatively few people who buy their homes are in a position to do so without a loan secured by a mortgage on their property. A house may well cost several times a person's annual income and, in any case, a high proportion of the income is needed for living expenses and other commitments.

Similarly, many businesses have to borrow to make substantial investments in premises and equipment (fixed assets in accounting parlance). The investment is intended to yield a profit, part of which will be required to meet repayment of the loan and the interest on it. The loan bridges the gap, therefore, between making the initial outlays and the generation of profits.

These two examples relate to long-term expenditures to acquire or create assets with lasting values. In all probability, a lender will examine carefully the suitability of the assets as security for a loan and the ability of the borrowers to repay within an agreed timescale. The process of borrowing and lending will be highly structured and supported by formal agreements.

By contrast, take the case of someone who has discovered the supposed freedom of credit cards to run up short-term debts beyond his means to service and repay. He gets to the point of desperation and asks a friend to lend him money. Even if the friend agrees to the request, what are the prospects of repayment of the private loan and what damage might a default inflict on the relationship?

I am confident that my parents would have excluded the two examples of long-term loans from the spirit of their saying. Their concern would have been my incurring short-term debts in an irresponsible way or my misguidedly trying to help out a friend in such a predicament. Because borrowing – or lending – involves risk, it is a serious decision and you should not let your heart rule your head. Give yourself space to weigh up carefully the pros and cons and to consider the fit within the great scheme of things.

In addition, risk features prominently in Chapters 6 and 8. Insurance is a way of sharing risk – at a cost – while prudent investors avoid putting all their eggs in one basket.

## some techniques

Three techniques that can help in assessing risk and in various other ways are (i) attention to detail, (ii) knowing one's strengths and weaknesses and (iii) adopting a sound framework for reaching decisions.

### attention to detail

Attention to detail is a hobby-horse fed, no doubt, by my 1960s training in a leading clearing bank.* It is a fundamental discipline and desirable regardless of how complicated your finances are proving to be. It involves reading the 'small print' and not cutting too many corners. I pursue the theme in Chapter 3 when I look at having a suitable bank account, monitoring your affairs and record-keeping.

### knowing one's strengths and weaknesses

Knowing one's strengths and weaknesses, particularly the limitations, is another helpful attribute. It can enhance decisions over whether or not to take professional advice and from whom, bearing in mind that there is likely to be a cost. Familiarity with one's rights as a buyer of personal financial services is a further safeguard and I return to topics such as these in Chapter 15.

### adopting a sound framework for reaching decisions

Last but not least comes adopting a sound framework for reaching decisions. Decision-making involves the exercise of judgement either on one's own or with the help of others. Reams have been written on the subject and, at its simplest, it boils down to a five-step process:

---

* According to the Collins English Dictionary [1979], a 'clearing bank' is 'any bank that makes use of the central clearing house in London for the transfer of credits and cheques between banks'. The definition predates the boom in electronic payments in recent years but, apart from that, is helpful. In practice, so-called clearing banks now combine their clearing functions with many others.

1  be clear about what you want to achieve;
2  obtain all the relevant information;
3  identify the possible courses of action;
4  evaluate and compare the benefits and drawbacks of each possibility;
5  make the decision and implement it.

## summary

I have conjured up a number of ideas in this section and here is a short summary of my recipe for achieving competence in personal finance:

- develop a feel for the subject and then focus on topics of relevance to you;
- always look at the downside, however attractive a proposition appears to be at first sight, and weigh the risks against the rewards;
- adopt a healthy attitude to borrowing and, if appropriate, to lending;
- watch the details, not least the 'small print';
- know your limitations and when to seek advice;
- make well-reasoned decisions.

The list is not exhaustive but I hope it provides food for thought.

## 1.3  having a sense of purpose

I have learned from hard experience the drawbacks of lacking direction in life. Equally, I have discovered the benefits of having a clear sense of purpose. Asserting the theory is one thing; putting it into practice is another.

Managing one's finances should not, in my view, be an end in itself. It is more a means to facilitate the achievement of the substantive purposes in life. For instance, if you want to develop a career, it helps to qualify in higher education. To do so, you need to pay your way; raising sufficient finance and deploying it effectively can mean the difference between success and failure.

Someone might say that his main aim in life is to get rich. I imagine a lot people would like to do so but one's aspirations need to be realistic and attainable. How are you to set about it? How long will it take? They are just two questions that call for considered answers.

Relying on a windfall such as a win on the Premium Bonds or the National Lottery is hardly realistic. The odds are far too long and you have little control over the process. On the other hand, entering a career for which you are well equipped and working steadily up the promotion ladder may enable you to enjoy a fulfilling working life and secure a comfortable lifestyle in retirement. The primary driver is the career; the shrewd management of your income and expenditure contributes to meeting your ambitions.

The prospect of planning ahead forty years or more is daunting. When I joined a bank the day after my twentieth birthday, the staff manager remarked that it was the ideal start date for my pension. Retirement had not crossed my mind until then and I thought he was mad! Now that I am in receipt of my pension, I can recognise better the workings of a shrewd mind.

A question posed on management courses is 'how do you eat an elephant?' and the answer is something like 'break it down into manageable bites.' You analyse the various components of the problem and then tackle ('eat') each one in turn. Thus you avoid being overwhelmed by something that is far too big to handle in one fell swoop.

Planning your personal finances for the next few decades is akin to trying to eat an elephant. You have an idea of where you want to end up but getting there will be a long and tortuous process. As an initial step, it is useful to analyse the sort of issues that you will need to address sooner or later but start only with those that call for immediate attention.

An outline biography of a typical man or woman may fall into the following seven phases. Each phase relates to an age range that is likely to coincide with major life events.

| Phase | Age | Life events | Financial position |
|---|---|---|---|
| 1 | Up to 18 | School education | Reliant on parents and casual earnings for upkeep and pocket money |
| 2 | 19–22 | Higher education | Needs to manage own expenditure<br>Reliant on parental allowance, casual earnings and student debt |
| 3 | 23–30 | Gap year<br>Starts work<br>Moves out from family home<br>Buys own house (on mortgage)<br>Marries (or equivalent)<br>Gets established in career | Poverty followed by reasonable earnings that increase steadily<br>Repayment of student debt<br>Responsibilities and commitments grow<br>Need for long-term provision |
| 4 | 31–40 | Young children<br>Self or partner leaves work temporarily or indefinitely<br>Working parent continues up career ladder | Good income but high commitments<br>Income reduced if one partner not earning |
| 5 | 41–55 | Children become more expensive, especially if in higher education<br>High earnings; both partners working | High earnings and high outgoings<br>May be potential for some savings |

| 6 | 56–65 | Parental responsibilities end | Earnings peak – plenty of scope for saving |
| | | Support for elderly parents (mainly practical) | Transition to pension |
| | | | Possible inheritance |
| | | Retirement | |
| 7 | Over 65 | Retired | Comfortable or well-off |
| | | Plenty of leisure time and travel | Commitments increase if unable to continue in own home |
| | | Own health considerations | |

Most major life events carry financial implications of one sort or another. Starting work, gaining a promotion and the death of a parent may, on the face of it, be beneficial to your financial wellbeing. Entering higher education, buying a house, having children and retiring from paid employment present financial challenges through increased commitments or a reduction in income.

An aim of managing one's finances is to be in a position to cope with setbacks if and when they occur. There are in each phase risks that may be identified and provided for. Obvious examples in phases 4 and 5 are loss of earnings through illness or the onset of disability.

I confess to never having mapped out a plan for my life on these lines. If I had at age 21, it would probably have been something like the one above minus the gap year in phase 3 (a rarity in my day). My own financial planning has often been reactive rather than proactive and, if things have turned out reasonably well, it has been as much by luck as good judgement. Even so, I might well have avoided many mistakes if I had been working to a coherent plan.

Experience tells me that it is healthy to have a long-term view of what you want to do with your life, both your working life and beyond, and the longer the view the better. At the same time, it is important to recognise that things may change for reasons within or beyond your control so your perspective needs flexibility.

I believe too that it is for each of us to do what we can to make our dreams a reality. Many things are beyond our control but we can all help to make our own luck. I do not want to overemphasise the monetary side but the quality of financial management is a factor that can make or break a business, voluntary organisation or individual.

My skeleton biography could be a young person's vision for his life. It is also a tool that I return to later to help illustrate the application of theory to practice in terms of personal finance.

Coming back to the elephant, however, it can be hard to look more than a few years ahead. Looming examinations will be foremost in the mind of a fifteen-year-old who will also be encouraged to consider life after school. A university student will focus on his degree but against a backdrop of the world of work. Both are preoccupied with what is just ahead yet conscious no doubt that further challenges lie beyond.

How far ahead can and should one plan? There is no right or wrong answer but my suggestion is to concentrate on the phase you are in but be preparing for the next one at least. It applies to both life events and the attendant financial consequences.

There is at least one aspect, however, that warrants a much longer view on current wisdom and that is providing for retirement. I expand on the subject later but there is a lot to be said for planning an income in retirement as early as one reasonably can. Looking ahead thirty or even forty years is not out of place.

Two great financial issues confronting the nation are the level of personal savings and meeting the cost of future pensions. Both, in my view, boil down to the same thing. We as a nation are spending more of our income on current consumption and setting aside less for the future. The charity Credit Action has published figures that show total personal debt standing at over £1¼ trillion at the end of October 2006 and that it was more than 2½ times the level of ten years earlier. This indicates an increase in debt averaging about 10 per cent a year – more than double the average rate of wage inflation. Can we continue to spend as we do in the short term and, at the same time, secure our long-term aspirations for a healthy standard of living? I have my doubts.

The view is controversial among economists, journalists and politicians, and time will tell whether it is alarmist or justified. In the meantime, it falls to individual temperament to decide how much is factored into one's financial plans for immediate spending and how much is tucked away for a rainy day. It is, however, just one of the decisions we have to make in the management of our personal finances.

To summarise:

- it helps to know your direction in life generally and, broadly, how you intend to pursue it;
- 'money' can facilitate achieving aims and plans but is not an end in itself;
- it is easier to react to events if you have been proactive in your financial planning.

# money and other expressions

introduction – money – cash – saving – investment–income–capital – income: earned and
unearned – expenditure – debts, liabilities – wealth – short, medium and long term – liquidity –
current assets and fixed assets – chattels – masculine and feminine – basis of law

## 2.1 introduction

Many of the expressions that I use are capable of more than one shade of
meaning and the purpose of this section is to reduce the risk of ambiguity by
clarifying what I intend.

## 2.2 money

Money is a classic case. If you look in a good dictionary, you will see a string
of definitions. It is not unusual, for instance, to say that someone has a lot of
money. You may well mean that the person is rich in relation to his total wealth
whatever form it takes. Alternatively, to say that he has not got any money may
mean that he does not have any currency (notes and coins) readily available. He
may, however, have a healthy balance on his bank account and merely need to
make a withdrawal.

Economists can have a field day with money and its functions as a medium
of exchange, store of value, and so on. It is all good stuff but unduly complicated
for the matter in hand.

I primarily use the term 'money' to mean something that you can spend
reasonably easily, such as the currency in your pocket and the credit balance
on your bank account. In other words, money is your own resources that are
readily convertible into goods and services.

This definition excludes credit card accounts on which you run up a debit
balance although they amount to 'near money'. Cheques, debit cards and credit
cards are not themselves money but devices to transfer it.

10

## 2.3 cash

**Cash** is to all intents and purposes currency. Bank accounts are sometimes referred to as **cash at bank** and credit balances are **near cash** even if not strictly cash. For convenience, I treat cash as both currency and an available balance on a bank current account.

## 2.4 saving

The idea of **saving** is to put money aside for spending in the future. **Savings** are the money so earmarked such as in a bank or building society deposit account or even in a tin box under the bed.

## 2.5 investment – income – capital

With **investment**, money is spent on an asset with a view to a profit such as a regular return of **income**. The form of an income varies according to the type of investment. For instance, a deposit yields **interest**, shares produce **dividends**, land and property yields **rent**.

The underlying investment is known as the **capital** and another form of profit is a **capital gain**, i.e. an increase in value of the underlying investment regardless of whether or not it is generating income. There is always a risk of a loss instead of a profit and the skill of investing involves judgement over prospective returns.

Investors often intend to keep their investments for several years. An investor can also hold his funds on a bank or building society deposit where there is a negligible risk of a capital loss but no question of a capital profit. For instance, an investor might choose to keep money on a deposit pending a decision over a longer-term investment or for reasons of timing.

Savers who do not intend to spend their savings for several years may choose to invest their savings in the hope of producing a capital gain as well as income. Hence there can be a fine distinction between savings and investment and the terms are often used interchangeably.

## 2.6 income: earned and unearned

A person's total income may be derived from several sources. There is a broad distinction between **earned** and **unearned** income. The former relates to income from employment or, if the person has his or her own business, from self-employment. The latter is mainly the income accruing from investments such as interest, dividends and rents.

## 2.7 expenditure

**Expenditure** or **spending** involves the payment of money or money's worth. You can spend money on consumer **goods** or **services** such as food, clothing, gas, electricity and telephone calls so that, once you have used them, you have nothing to show for your expenditure. Alternatively, you can spend money to acquire a house to live in or as an investment. In such a case, you are swapping your money for another asset that you hope will retain its value.

Certain types of asset tend to fall between these two extremes. You will expect a motor car to last you for several years but it is a depreciating asset in the sense that its value falls away over time. The same is true of furniture and household appliances.

There are, nonetheless, exceptions to the general rule. Some enthusiasts buy classic cars, works of art, jewellery, etc in the hope that they can both enjoy them and make a profit. They need to bear in mind the costs of ownership (such as maintenance, storage and insurance) and probably no income from the assets to defray them.

## 2.8 debts, liabilities

In assessing wealth (see below), it is usual to deduct the monetary value of financial obligations such as **debts** or **liabilities**. There are arguably different shades of meaning for debts and liabilities but both relate to money that you owe. Hence I am treating them as synonomous.

Debts may be obvious in the sense that you have run up a bill with your credit card or have not paid your Council Tax. There can also be contingent or latent liabilities; for example, if you sell an asset at a profit, the transaction might trigger to a liability to Capital Gains Tax (CGT).

## 2.9 wealth

**Wealth** denotes the totality of your assets. They will usually be valued in monetary terms for tax or other purposes.

Some valuations are relatively easy to make or ascertain. For example, a bank deposit of £10,000 encashable at short notice is usually worth £10,000; it might be worth considerably less, on the other hand, if the bank gets into difficulties. The price of shares in a company traded on a stock exchange can be highly volatile but the current price is easily ascertained.

The current value of assets such as land and buildings or the contents of a house can be more problematic. It is often possible to come up with a reasonable estimate but, on occasion, it will be necessary to obtain a formal valuation from a suitable expert.

Your **gross wealth** is your total assets before taking off your known total debts (liabilities). Your **net wealth** is assets minus liabilities and is negative if the liabilities exceed the assets.

I have adopted a material perspective in relation to wealth. At a spiritual level, one might place more emphasis on the wonders of nature but such an approach would be out of place in a book about personal finance!

## 2.10  short, medium and long term

Returning to practicality, it is worth comparing **short term** with **long term**, the gap between them being **medium term**. They are concepts rather than precise definitions and the point when short becomes medium and medium comes long is likely to vary with the circumstances. As a general proposition, however, up to one year is often regarded as short term, over five years long term and one to five years is medium term. A significant exception to this rule of thumb relates to 'dated' British Government securities; please see also Section 4.5.

## 2.11  liquidity

Time is also a characteristic of **liquidity** and **illiquidity. Liquid assets** are money and other assets that can readily be turned into money. A no-notice bank deposit is pretty liquid; a seven-day-notice account is fairly liquid; a deposit fixed for two years is relatively illiquid. A fixed deposit may become liquid if you accept the price of a penalty for early access to it.

Shares quoted on a stock exchange can be sold at short notice and the proceeds should be available within a few days. To that extent, the shares are relatively liquid but the sale may be at a bad time.

By contrast, assets such as land and buildings can be highly illiquid. There may not be willing buyers even at a low price and the procedure to complete a sale can take several weeks or months.

## 2.12  current assets and fixed assets

Two terms used in accounting are current assets and fixed assets and I use them in fairly similar senses. I treat current assets as money (as I have defined it above) and any sums receivable in the near future (e.g. unpaid earnings, repayment of Income Tax). Fixed assets, on the other hand, are your home (if you own it) and savings and investments that, ideally, you do not want to dip into for many years if at all.

Current assets are liquid whereas fixed assets tend to be illiquid. Also, you can convert current assets into fixed ones and fixed assets into current ones.

## 2.13  chattels

A collective term for tangible possessions such as a car, furniture, clothes and other personal items is chattels and it can be a moot point whether they are 'fixed' or 'current'. For simplicity, I regard them as fixed in that they are necessary for day-to-day living and, if they wear out, you will probably replace them.

## 2.14  masculine and feminine

I generally treat 'he', 'his' and similar expressions as incorporating the feminine as well as the masculine. It is purely for convenience and not evidence of male chauvinism.

## 2.15 basis of law

I have based the text on the law of England and Wales. Most legal systems, including that in Scotland, have equivalent concepts but there can be notable differences of law and practical effect. I assume too that people involved are 'UK residents' for tax and other purposes.

chapter **3**

the basic tools

introduction – banking – monitoring – record-keeping – minimising your expenditure, maximising your income

## 3.1 introduction

Four important tools or techniques in the management of your finances are (i) operating a suitable bank account, (ii) monitoring your financial position, (iii) keeping meaningful records and (iv) minimising your expenditure and maximising your income.

## 3.2 banking

Most people have a bank account nowadays. Long gone are the days when workers collected their wages in cash weekly and it would be difficult to exist without a bank account for many reasons. An initial question is what sort of account to open and with which organisation.

### banks

An obvious organisation is a **bank**. There are, however, many categories of bank including clearing banks, merchant banks, private banks and investment banks; several banking groups combine many if not all of these functions.

Yet another category is **mortgage banks**. This category has arisen largely through building societies converting themselves into banks or being taken over by banks. **Building societies** were traditionally mutual ventures that advanced loans on mortgage primarily for house purchase. They financed their lending by taking in deposits on which they paid interest but at rates lower than on their loans. Until **demutualisation**, their owners were in effect their **members**, i.e. depositors and borrowers. A few building societies remain as mutual organisations but the movement is a shadow of its former self.

Most people opt for a **high street bank**, essentially a bank in the business of retail banking with branches on the high street. Even so, you can now conduct much of your banking by post, telephone or via the Internet. Most of the leading players offer a wide range of delivery methods albeit they are encouraging their customers to embrace the newer ones.

## what you need

Whatever the means of operation, you need a current account for your day-to-day transactions, i.e. for the collection and deposit of income and other credit items and for the disbursement of outgoings by cheque, plastic debit card, standing order, direct debit, etc. Whether or not you need a separate deposit account depends on the amount of spare money you have. You can open a deposit account with the provider of your current account or look to other organisations that might pay a better rate of interest.

Banking is a highly competitive business and there is a plethora of accounts available. The trick is to find something that is suitable for your particular requirements. Charges for the use of cash machines and for other transactions that you are likely to incur warrant investigation and comparison. The rates of credit and debit interest may also be material.

The banks are generally anxious to attract students and many offer interest-free overdraft facilities up to certain limits. For someone that expects to operate in credit with a sizeable balance, on the other hand, credit interest rates are an important consideration.

There may also be all sorts of inducements to open an account, such as the offer of free travel insurance and discounts on holidays and other goods and services for as long as the account remains open. Such peripheral attractions need to be evaluated carefully. The prime consideration is a suitable account; if the additions make the offer more attractive, all well and good, but genuine 'free lunches' are rare in my experience.

## credit cards

Credit cards are, of course, separate from bank accounts and it is not necessary to obtain them from your main banker. Whereas a current account is a must for most people, credit cards are essentially an optional extra. They are a means of borrowing money but they provide other facilities such as a convenient way of making payments with the benefit of a period of interest-free credit. I return to their merits and demerits in Chapter 5.

Occupational hazards with modern banking are the complex processes to open an account and trying to remember a portfolio of PINs (personal identity numbers). There are good reasons for all the security but one can easily lose sight of it when grappling with the bureaucracy.

## prepaid payment cards

A variation on plastic cards that is becoming popular is prepaid payment cards. They are loaded with money and can be used to buy goods and services or for withdrawals of cash from, for example, ATMs (automatic teller machines). They are distinct from debit and credit cards in that there is no element of credit – you cannot overdraw them – and are more easily obtainable in that respect. They are more secure than cash as they are normal operated on a PIN and are replaceable if mislaid. A useful application is for taking foreign currency on a trip abroad. A health warning relates to the costs; they can be significant.

## 3.3 monitoring

As a general proposition, you should review all aspects of your personal finances periodically. My immediate concern is with keeping track of one's bank balance but I cover other aspects in later sections.

The idea is partly to make sure that what comes in is sufficient to cover what goes out and partly to check that the transactions passed through your account are correct. Two essential qualities are (i) developing a sound method and (ii) the discipline of keeping your accounting up to date.

### method

As to method, it is for the individual to discover what is best for him and, if my experience is any thing to go by, there will be improvements and refinements as one gets used to the process. An obvious consideration is whether to (i) keep handwritten records or (ii) use a proprietory package or a spreadsheet of your own design on a personal computer. The choice depends on factors such as the complexity of one's finances and one's familiarity with computer software. Sound design and method are critical and thinking the process through at the outset is time well spent.

### budget

If you are starting from scratch and particularly if money is tight, preparation of a budget is a must. A budget is an estimate of income and expenditure and is a recognised technique of financial management for business concerns, voluntary organisations and individuals. The concept is similar for each and it is only the details which differ.

It is usual to budget on an annual basis but there can be good reasons for adopting a longer or shorter period. For instance, an undergraduate might want to budget ahead for the prospective three years of his university course but with a subdivision into years or terms. If a crisis arises, it may be worth concentrating on getting through the next few months but with a weather eye on the longer term. It is essential to react to changes in circumstances and to do so promptly.

What should go into a budget? Broadly, there are two columns, one for projected income and the other for projected expenditure for the period of account. The idea is to check that the total income at least matches the total expenditure and, if it does not, to consider ways to deal with the shortfall.

## money in

The sources of income include earnings and investment income such as rents from tenanted properties, dividends on shares, and interest on securities and deposit accounts. An allowance from a parent or other relative is another possible source of income.

The receipt of a loan is not strictly income. A loan is a method of financing expenditure for which funds are not otherwise available. Loans have to be repaid eventually although, as in the case of student loans, repayment may be deferred for several years. In the meantime, the loan helps balance the accounts and may appear as a receipt rather than income.

## money out

Turning to expenditure, it is important to identify all outgoings that are a claim against income. Legal, moral and social obligations should be accounted for.

Legal obligations include a contractual duty to make payments for goods or services. They also cover the payment of tax and of maintenance arising from the breakdown of a marriage.

Moral obligations encompass responsibilities for the wellbeing of close members of the family. As far as spouses and children are concerned, there can be a fine distinction between legal and moral obligations. Legal obligations are more tenuous in relation to unmarried partners and others such as elderly parents unable to fend for themselves.

Social obligations relate more to people and causes beyond the family circle. A high proportion of community work is down to the efforts of the so-called voluntary sector. Charities are a key component of the sector but rely on the donations of their supporters. Similarly, the international aid charities appeal to the general public at times of disaster in the Third World or even in more developed countries.

Legal, moral and social commitments are actual or potential claims against income and, ideally, one should provide for them fully before indulging in other things. The term 'commitment' is of course open to interpretation, especially in moral and social matters. Once there is a commitment, however, it should be met and, if need be, sacrifices should be made accordingly.

## capital transactions

Certain transactions are by nature capital and should normally be excluded from a budget of income and expenditure. I am thinking, for example, of the sale of one asset (such as shares in company A) and the reinvestment of the proceeds in another (perhaps shares in company B). The situation would be different if you were selling an asset to top up your income. In this case, the receipt might justifiably appear in the budget but as a one-off rather than normal income. Similarly, if you were investing surplus income, the expenditure side could show the application as an exceptional item.

## income and expenditure, receipts and payments

Income and expenditure relate to what are due for the period. Receipts and payments, on the other hand, represent what is actually received or paid during the period irrespective of whether they are due in that period or another. For example, you may be working to the calendar year but an income receipt due on 15 December may not come in until 12 January in the following year. The timing does not affect the income due but it can have implications for the cash in hand. You may be due to make a payment on 31 December but have you sufficient in your bank account to do so before 12 January?

## timing

Timing introduces the idea of keeping sufficient in hand to meet outgoings as and when they are due. One method is a working balance on your bank account in case it is necessary to pay outgoings before the corresponding income is available. Another is temporary borrowing such as by overdraft on a bank current account or by use of a credit card. There may of course be a cost to borrowing in the form of interest charges and arrangement fees.

The size of a working balance or loan finance will depend largely on the patterns of receipts and payments. If a budget extends to a year, I advise breaking it down into shorter periods, preferably months. Many forms of income and expenditure follow a monthly pattern and are easily tracked. Watch out, however, for the exceptions such as insurance premiums where the entire amount is payable annually in advance.

Many suppliers offer a facility to pay in monthly instalments by direct debit. Where such facility is offered, it is worth considering if only from the point of view of simplifying cash management. Some power utilities encourage monthly direct debits by a small discount from the bill. Others, such as insurance companies, may levy an interest charge.

## rules of thumb

In making all these calculations, I suggest working in reasonably round figures (i.e. to the nearest few pounds rather than pence) and erring on the side of caution. The cautious approach is to pitch estimates low for income and high for expenditure. If you are uncertain about an income receipt, reduce it or omit it completely. With expenditure, provide for it generously even if it may not arise.

Ownership of a house or a car carries a responsibility to keep it in good repair or working order. Some outgoings such as insurance premiums and servicing costs (for a car especially) are reasonably predictable. Others occur unexpectedly and often inconveniently. It is prudent to build something into your calculations for the unknown or unpredictable.

I have concentrated so far in this section on formulating a budget in order to assess the likely balance between your income and your expenditure. I turn now to keeping abreast of what is happening in practice. If you are keeping reasonably in line with your budget, there should be no surprises. If not and a nasty surprise is looming, the quicker you get on to it the better.

You need to achieve two things:

1 check that you have sufficient in your bank account or elsewhere to pay your way;
2 be aware of any significant variations from your budget and the reasons why.

How you keep tabs depends on how you conduct your finances. If you have just one bank account and no credit card, the process should be relatively easy. If you have a combination of bank and credit card accounts, life is likely to be more complicated in that you need to consolidate all the information.

Whatever your method, you should arrange to receive regular statements, preferably monthly ones, and to file them in an orderly way. As a rule of thumb, I like to keep bank and other statements for at least six complete tax years, i.e. the year to 5 April. Partly also for tax reasons, I adopt the year to 31 March for my household accounts. A student, on the other hand, may prefer the year to 31 August or 30 September to coincide with the pattern of academic life. The calendar year will be convenient for many.

You should also check the statements for accuracy and, if you find any discrepancies, contact the bank or credit card company promptly. In order to carry out the checks, retain your transaction slips and, if you write cheques, complete the stubs with the date, payee and amount.

Whether or not you have prepared a formal budget, it is helpful to combine a check of the transactions on the statements with a review of your overall financial position, essentially a comparison of the funds available to you with your commitments. A simple review may take the form of totting up your balances as at the last day of each month and making adjustments for any overdue income or expenditure as well as any unbudgeted commitments.

You may wish to separate from the main analysis any receipts and payments of an exceptional nature that do not have a direct bearing on your budget. An example of an exceptional receipt might be the proceeds of a legacy that you wish to set aside for a rainy day. You are in effect treating the legacy as capital rather than income. Similarly, exceptional payments such as for buying a house are by nature capital as opposed to running expenditure.

If you have made a formal budget, it makes sense to complete the process by comparing the actual figures with the projected ones. You can only complete the comparison at the end of the period but you may wish to monitor progress in the meantime.

The ideas I have put forward are to help you to come up with a workable method of your own. It does not matter whether you prefer to use a computer or pencil and paper. The important thing is to devise something that is effective and meaningful to you.

I describe in Appendix A an analysis of the income and expenditure of a hypothetical married couple who conduct their finances through a bank account in their joint names. The format is suitable for both budgeting and monitoring and comprises columns for each month and a total for the entire year of account.

## 3.4 record-keeping

You can divide records into three broad categories:

- original documents
- important papers
- routine correspondence.

I use the term **original documents** to mean papers that have an inherent monetary value either directly or indirectly. They include the title deeds of a house, share and bond certificates, life assurance policies, your copy of a legal contract (e.g. for building works) and your will. Such items can be difficult to replace and should be kept in a safe place and, where possible, in secure, fireproof conditions. Particularly with documents such as house deeds, I recommend their being kept out of the house and in the bank vault, even though a modest custody charge may be payable. You may wish to keep a working copy that is more readily available.

**Important papers** include bank statements, statements from other suppliers of financial services, dividend and interest warrants, other information required for a tax return and insurance policies (for house, car, etc.). Again, they should be kept in a safe place and preferably in secure conditions. You are likely to need the papers and I am mindful too of the increasing preoccupation with identity theft.

**Routine correspondence** is anything else. Twin considerations are keeping only as much as you need to and filing what you keep in a logical system or order. For example, with bonus notices on a with-profits policy, it is probably sufficient to keep merely the latest one and to discard the previous ones.

With computer records, for example your budget or household accounts, there may well be a facility to protect the files with a password. Remember too to make regular back-ups of material you do not wish to lose.

## 3.5 minimising your expenditure, maximising your income

Keeping your expenditure down and your income up are two ways of stretching your financial resources. You can tackle one or the other or, better still, both at the same time.

On the expenditure side, steps open to you are pretty obvious such as not buying so many goods and services or buying more cheaply. A sound test over how much to spend is 'value for money'. It may not necessarily be the cheapest option but rather the one which maximises the benefit of every £1 you spend.

For example, you can buy a cheap car. It may result in a relatively low initial outlay but, if it is heavy on fuel and costly to maintain, it may prove a bigger drain on your pocket over time than a model costing more at the outset. With commodities such as gas and electricity, on the other hand, all suppliers provide essentially the same thing subject to possible variations in service and reliability. By and large, therefore, you can look to the cheapest, although what is cheapest this quarter may not be so the next one!

Within the realms of personal finance, keeping borrowing costs to a minimum is a priority. The possibilities include borrowing less, switching providers (but watch the fees and commission on mortgages in particular) and switching credit type (for example, personal loans are generally cheaper than borrowing equivalent sums on a credit card). On the asset side, you can look for a better return by, for example, switching type of investment (but watch the risks) or changing supplier (such as moving a deposit account to a fresh deposit-taker).

Similarly, you can improve your income by working harder or by finding a better-paid job, perhaps because you have improved your qualifications. Another avenue is to ensure that you claim all that is due to you. This is particularly true of state benefits.

## claiming state benefits

The state provides benefits in a number of ways and several government agencies are involved. In broad terms, the responsibilities for welfare benefits are as follows:

▸ Jobcentre Plus run by the Department of Work and Pensions (DWP) – the local centres are generally the first port of call for claims of people of working age for jobseekers' allowance, statutory sick pay, incapacity benefit, income support, severe disablement allowance, etc.
▸ The Pension Service (DWP) – state retirement pension, pension credits for people over 60.
▸ Child Support Agency (DWP) – runs the child support system.
▸ Disability and Carers Service (DWP) – supports disabled people and their carers though attendance allowance, disability living allowance and carer's allowance.
▸ Her Majesty's Revenue and Customs (HMRC) – as well as operating the taxation system, it is responsible for child tax credit, working tax credit, child benefit and guardian's allowance.
▸ Local authorities – housing benefit, council tax benefit.

Social care falls largely to local authorities through their Social Services Departments and covers support arising from age, illness and disability. The

National Health Service (NHS) is responsible for medical and health care issues and operates mainly through Strategic Health Authorities, Primary Care Trusts and Secondary Care Trusts.

There is a considerable volume of resources to help you find your way around and I refer you to Further reading and resources. For more information on welfare benefits for the elderly, see also Chapter 13.

chapter **4**

# Common forms of wealth

introduction – currency – bank and building society deposits – National Savings and Investments – loan stocks – land and buildings – tangible possessions – business interests – company shares – life assurance products – pension rights – intellectual property – derivatives and hedge funds

## 4.1  introduction

I have used the term 'wealth' in previous sections and the point of this chapter is to examine ways in which wealth may be held or owned. I have discussed cash and bank and building society deposits but include them here to help comparison with other classes of assets. I concentrate on assets that one is most likely to encounter in practice and hence the coverage is not exhaustive.

## 4.2  currency

I refer particularly to sterling notes and coins in ordinary circulation. Modern currency has a negligible intrinsic value and cannot be exchanged nowadays for its equivalent in gold or other precious metals. It relies on general acceptance for its value. The same is true of the currencies of other nations such as US dollars and the euro in circulation in many of the EU countries.

Cash in the form of currency is useful for small transactions but is otherwise an unattractive way of holding wealth. It does not earn interest and is vulnerable to theft or loss.

## 4.3  bank and building society deposits

Traditionally, banks and building societies were very different animals but the distinction has become somewhat blurred in recent years. As noted in Chapter 5, a number of building societies have converted to banks and others have been taken over by banks. The principal objective of building societies was to provide long-term finance for house purchase and to attract deposits for this purpose.

Banks provided current accounts for day-to-day financial transactions. They did not normally pay interest on such accounts and levied transaction charges (known as bank charges). They paid interest on standard deposit accounts for which seven days' notice of withdrawal was required.

An interest-bearing deposit with a bank or building society is essentially a loan to the institution. Hence, a depositor is concerned with the financial strength of the deposit-taker – he wants his money back in due course – as well as the rate of interest. Interest is the reward for allowing use of the money.

The term of a deposit, i.e. the period to its repayment date, may vary from withdrawals on demand or on the expiry of a period of notice (e.g. 30 days) to a fixed date (e.g. one year after the deposit was made). As a general proposition, the longer the term of the deposit, the higher the rate of interest. In practice, the differentials may be insignificant, especially when interest rates are low, and longer-term deposits can even attract lower rates than shorter-term ones if there is an expectation that interest rates will fall.

The rate of interest may be fixed or variable. A term deposit (e.g. of one year) generally carries a fixed rate for the term. Short or no-notice deposits carry variable rates; the deposit-taker adjusts his rates according to the prevailing market conditions. With tracker accounts, the rates are generally set at a margin below an independent rate (e.g. the Bank of England base rate).

Modern banking may be conducted in various ways including through the high street branches, by post, by telephone and via the Internet. Banks and building societies are keen to minimise their running costs so deposits through 'remote' banking tend to attract better rates of interest than branch-based ones.

There is an official deposit protection scheme for depositors so that, subject to limits, their money is recoverable should the deposit-taker default on its obligations. The Financial Services Compensation Scheme runs it and I show in Section 15.3 the maximum compensation that can be claimed.

The scheme is not something I would wish to rely on as there could be an extensive delay in recouping one's funds and, no doubt, significant paperwork in sustaining one's claim. Hence I am wary of placing money with little-known organisations or ones offering spectacular terms. Where large sums are involved, there might be merit in spreading funds with two or more reputable deposit-takers even if it entails a small loss of interest. From a practical point of view, I find it inconceivable that a household name would be allowed to go bust; it would rock the financial system in this country and possibly others throughout the world!

A variation on the theme of deposits is **structured products** one form of which is **guaranteed equity bonds**. These instruments are a form of deposit on which the return (i.e. interest) is linked to the performance of a stock market during the term of the bond, e.g. five years. Withdrawals are not usually allowed during the term. It is essential to examine such products carefully and to understand the risks. With some versions, for instance, there can be a loss of the money originally deposited if there is a sustained fall in the stock market.

It is a classic example of where you should read the small print and not cut corners.

A deposit itself is not liable to fluctuations in value in monetary terms. It is, however, vulnerable to erosion in purchasing power (or real value) through inflation as the monetary cost of goods and services tends to rise.

## 4.4 National Savings and Investments

National Savings and Investments (NS&I) is the trade mark of the Director of Savings, a government official responsible for attracting finance for the government from individuals. The various NS&I products are tantamount to loans to the government so that default is inconceivable.

The headline rates of interest tend to be relatively low but are often boosted by tax incentives. There are limits on how much an individual can invest and some products are restricted to particular categories of investor (e.g. children, pensioners).

The range includes Premium Savings Bonds and National Savings Certificates (fixed-interest and index-linked). Premium Bonds, which award prizes rather than offering a rate of interest, may be held indefinitely whereas Savings Certificates are for fixed terms, generally up to five years. The NS&I website www.nsandi.com gives up-to-date information.

As with bank and other deposits, the capital values are fixed in monetary terms so their purchasing power is vulnerable to the effects of inflation. The idea of index-linked products is to counteract the effects of inflation in the prices of consumer goods.

## 4.5 loan stocks

A **loan stock** is a loan to the government, to another public institution such as a local authority or to a company in private (as opposed to public) ownership. The borrower may require the finance for a specific purpose such as, in the case of the government, the nationalisation of an industry or, in the case of a company, the acquisition of another company. Loan stocks are often called **bonds** although that term may also mean other things.

The term of the loan will usually be several years and the prospectus issued in connection with the stock will identify the proposed means of repayment. There tends to be a single rate of interest for the whole term of the loan based on the general level of interest rates at the time of issue, the perceived financial strength of the borrower and the extent of any specific security for the loan.

**Undated** stocks have no set date for redemption but are repayable at the behest of the borrower. A classic example is the British Government's $3^1/_2\%$ War Loan that originates from the First World War. As far as **dated** government stocks are concerned, ones with up to 5 years to redemption have traditionally been viewed as short-dated, those with 5–15 years to run as medium-dated and those with over 15 years to run as long-dated. Some editions of the Financial

Times (FT) newspaper now group them into 'shorts', 5–10 years, 10–15 years and over 15 years when publishing their prices and other information.

Government loan stocks are secured on the general revenues of the Government, notably taxation, and are regarded as of the highest quality in terms of security. Hence they are termed **gilt-edged securities** or 'gilts' for short. Other names include **government bonds** and **treasury bonds**. Company loan stocks are also termed **corporate bonds**.

The Government has issued over the years a number of **index-linked** stocks in respect of which the half-yearly interest payments and the eventual repayment of capital are adjusted with movements in the (Government's) Retail Prices Index (RPI). These stocks are known as **index-linked gilts**.

Company loan stocks are seen as less secure than gilts and hence carry a higher rate of interest to counteract the extra risk. There have, over the years, been failures that have resulted in investors losing all or part of their money.

Company loan stocks may be **secured** or **unsecured**. All stocks are secured in the sense that they are debts of the company and loan stockholders rank as general creditors to the extent that their stock is not specifically secured (i.e. unsecured). The stockholders are in a stronger position if their claims are supported by a charge (or mortgage) over specific assets such as land, buildings and fixtures; they have first bite of the cherry (i.e. those assets) should the company cease to trade. Much can hinge of course on the marketable value of the secured assets if it comes to the crunch.

Government and other loan stocks are quoted on the London Stock Exchange and may be bought and sold by investors prior to redemption (repayment) of the stock. The capital value tends to fluctuate over the life of the stock for a number of reasons so that an investor does not have a guaranteed capital value until the borrower finally repays.

A few companies have issued **convertible loan stocks** that give a right to convert the loan stock into shares in the company on specified terms and on stipulated dates. The price of the loan stock is usually influenced by the price of the company's shares as conversion dates approach.

Generally, loan stocks are vulnerable to inflation, although index-linked gilts are designed to give some protection in this respect. I return to the subject of loan stocks in Chapter 8.

## 4.6 land and buildings

The subject of land and the law relating to it is involved and the following remarks are no more than a flavour of its scope. Land is just one of the names used; another is **real estate**.

An owner-occupier of land normally owns the buildings erected on it, fences, trees, crops and **fixtures and fittings** attached to the buildings in particular. A fixture or fitting is something like a fitted wardrobe built into the fabric of the building whereas a free-standing cupboard placed in a bedroom is a piece of furniture and not a fixture or fitting of the land.

A touring caravan parked for convenience on the drive is not part of the land. On the other hand, the position may be different with a static caravan that is fastened to the land and linked to the services (electricity, water, drainage, etc.).

There have also to be qualifications on the extent of ownership. There are general exclusions for mineral rights on or beneath the surface and for the air space above the land. The land may also be subject to the specific rights of others, e.g. for legitimate passage across the land or to prevent unsociable activities on the land.

A **freeholder** owns the land in perpetuity and, as with other assets, can leave it by will to his heirs. A **leaseholder**, on the other hand, has his interest in the land for a specific term, e.g. 7 years, 21 years, 99 years or even 999 years. He pays a rent to the freeholder, or a superior leaseholder, during the term and his ownership is subject to conditions known as **covenants**. Typical covenants include an agreement to pay the rent, repairing obligations and constraints on the use to which the land may be put. **Rent** is the reward for allowing use of the premises.

A **tenant** is one entitled to occupy land under a lease such as I have described or under some sort of tenancy agreement. For instance, a tenancy agreement from year to year continues until properly ended by one of the parties. The law has a lot of say in how interests in land may be created, transferred and ended and carries considerable protections for tenants in particular.

It follows that an owner of land may occupy it himself or allow someone else the use of it for payment of rent. An owner of a house may occupy it as his own residence or let it to tenants. In the latter case, he probably regards the house as an investment.

The subject of land is complicated further by the many different uses to which it may be put. Residential property is self-explanatory and covers houses, flats and apartments. Commercial property is often subdivided into retail, offices and industrial. Trading concerns often prefer to rent rather than own their premises. Much commercial property is owned, therefore, by property investment concerns and institutions such as pension funds.

Farmland, moorland, heathland and woodland amount to a significant proportion of the country but investing in them is highly specialised. Estates tend to be large and sizeable sums are required to achieve a reasonable investment.

Owning your own home is a basic form of security and can be an excellent way of building a nest egg for old age or passing it on to the next generation. You have to bear in mind, however, the costs of a mortgage, repairs, improvements, heat, light, power and council tax. Your own home is not generally a convenient way to generate income and people often end up with a lot of wealth tied up in bricks and mortar and a shortage of ready money.

Historically, house prices have tended to rise in line with people's earnings. The value of other premises is governed by many factors, not least the general strength of the economy. Property markets of all types, however, are prone to imbalances between demand and supply and, consequently, to periods of boom and bust.

As an investment, land is just one of a range of possibilities and should be evaluated accordingly. I return to the subject in Chapter 8.

## 4.7 tangible possessions

**Tangible possessions** are things that you can see, feel, touch, use, etc. In Chapter 2, I defined chattels as items such as a car, furniture, clothes and other artefacts for personal use. Some people regard certain tangible goods, e.g. paintings, stamps, fine wines, as investments rather than chattels. Their primary motive in ownership is a monetary gain as opposed to personal use and enjoyment.

Tangibles may also be classed as **business assets**, e.g. plant and machinery, tools and equipment, cars and vans. A car may, therefore, serve as a chattel for personal use, may be classed as a business asset or may combine the two uses.

Considerations over ownership include facilites for storage, the costs of maintenance and insurance and the absence of a ready market for many items.

Houses and flats are sometimes let on a furnished basis in which case part of the rent is strictly attributable to the contents.

## 4.8 business interests

Many people who go into business on their own account, i.e. do not work for an employer, do so as **sole traders**. They alone own the assets of the business, e.g. tools, van, premises, and are directly responsible for the liabilities of the business, e.g. bank loan, claims of customers for damages. The **net worth** of the business is its assets minus the liabilities. An important asset of a business may be an intangible asset known as **goodwill**, broadly a value placed on the reputation of the business.

A sole trader may employ other people in his business. Subject to the payment of the employees' wages, he remains entitled to the profits of the business and is responsible for the liabilities. Potential liabilities and responsibilities may increase significantly as a result of employing others.

If two or more people engage in a business and share the profits and liabilities, they are said to be **partners**. They should ideally set out their respective rights and responsibilities in a formal partnership agreement. Partners need not be equal. In a partnership comprising members of the same family, the father may be the **senior partner** with a bigger share of the profits than his children.

The value of a business can be governed by many factors but profitability, the quality of management and reputation are key if the business is to be sold as a going concern.

## 4.9 company shares

A company is a legal entity separate from those who own it. The owners' entitlement is divided up into **shares** and the owners are **shareholders**; they share in the fortunes of the company. There may be more than one class of shares and, if so, the rights and obligations of each class will differ. Almost invariably, there will be a class of **ordinary shares**.

Shares generally carry the right to **dividends** paid out of the company's **profits** while the company is in existence. The profits are what remain of the company's revenues after all its expenses have been accounted for. The expenses include any interest on borrowings. Profits may be retained in the company, paid out as dividends or, as is quite usual, partly retained and partly paid out.

The shareholders may decide to wind up or liquidate a company and creditors may be able to insist on it if the company is unable to pay its debts. The shareholders are entitled to what remains after all the legitimate claims of creditors and others have been met. If there is a shortfall, the creditors may lose out and the shareholders will receive nothing. If there is a surplus and there are two or more classes of share, the priority between classes is determined by the company's constitution.

Companies are also known as **corporations** or **corporate bodies** whereas sole traders and partnerships are **unincorporated**. The latter conduct business in their own right, whereas with companies, ownership and business entity are kept separate.

There are various pros and cons of incorporation. Two important advantages of conducting a business through a company are that:

‣ it facilitates a more diverse and fragmented ownership;
‣ the company itself rather than the shareholders is liable for the debts and other obligations of the business although there are exceptions and qualifications to this principle of **limited liability**.

Relatively small companies may be registered as **private** and carry the word 'limited' in their name, e.g. Joe Bloggs Limited. Larger companies, especially ones whose shares are traded on the London Stock Exchange, are subject to more onerous regulation and are styled **public limited company** or **plc**, e.g. The Royal Bank of Scotland Group plc.

There is a distinction between **trading companies** and **investment companies**. Trading companies produce goods or services and include entities such as manufacturers, oil producers, banks, insurers and hoteliers, to mention a few. Investment companies are not producers as such but often hold shares in other companies with a view to making a capital profit from selling the shares and receiving the dividend income in the meantime.

Property companies may **trade** in that they develop land and buildings or buy and sell properties to yield a return. Alternatively, they may **invest** in properties in that they hold them for their rental income and with the intention of a capital profit on an eventual sale.

Buying and selling shares, normally ones quoted on a securities market, is a risky venture. Prices may be subject to wide fluctuations, often as a result of factors not directly connected with the company itself. Even so, company share analysis is a complex yet fascinating subject and entails both quantitative and qualitative skills. I return to it in Chapter 9.

## 4.10  life assurance products

Life assurance products take a number of forms. There are protection policies that provide for payment of an amount in the event of the death of the life assured before a certain date. Others are primarily investment vehicles with an element of life assurance built in.

I deal with the subject in more detail in Chapters 6 and 8.

## 4.11  pension rights

The main object of participating in a pension scheme is to produce an income in retirement. There are, nonetheless, many variations on the theme and I devote Chapter 11 to the topic.

## 4.12  intellectual property

**Intellectual property** is a collective term for cerebral rights such as the copyright of authors, the performing and recording rights of composers and other artists, and the registered patent rights of inventors. It is public policy to grant the owners certain legal protections against the exploitation of their ideas and ingenuity without their permission.

The rights can be valuable in that an owner need only grant permission on payment of a fee or royalty. Legal protection is not absolute so that, for instance, the maximum copyright protection for authors is (at early 2007) for life plus 70 years, and patent rights on patentable inventions can be protected for up to 20 years.

Intellectual property is a highly specialised subject and I mention it purely for completeness.

## 4.13  derivatives and hedge funds

There is a range of financial instruments, often known as **derivatives**, that may offer attractive returns but are highly risky in the hands of the uninitiated. I have in mind the likes of warrants, futures, options, contracts for differences and spread betting.

Many are designed to exploit short-term movements in their respective markets. If the market moves against you, however, the results can be disastrous. Derivatives do not produce an income such as interest and some can involve personal liability beyond the original commitment.

**Hedge funds** have increased in popularity in the last few years. They were once the preserve of the mega-rich but are becoming more accessible to the moderately wealthy. They are designed to act as a cushion against the swings in the normal securities markets and adopt a variety of strategies such as:

- aggressive use of derivatives
- borrowing heavily
- selling short (i.e. selling assets that they do not own) and buying them back after the price has dropped.

The theory sounds fine but, if you are tempted, I urge you to do your homework and bear firmly in mind that risk and reward tend to be closely related. Fee structures can be complicated and anecdotal evidence suggests that hedge fund management is often a lucrative business to be in.

Hence, derivatives and hedge funds come with a health warning in bold letters and are not for the novice or faint-hearted. I mention them mainly for completeness.

borrowing

introduction – a lender's point of view – sources of finance – servicing costs – health warnings – checklist

## 5.1 introduction

You will have gathered from my remarks in Section 1.2 that I am wary about borrowing. That is of course a personal view and attitudes towards credit and borrowing have changed considerably in the last few decades. Personal debt stands at unprecedented levels and has enabled people to enjoy consumer goods and services far sooner than if they had had to save up.

Borrowing has fuelled economic growth and hence contributed directly to the wealth of the nation. Much business investment would not have been possible without generous lines of credit and buoyant consumer expenditure has, at times, helped the economy keep its head above water. They are some of the positives in the explosion of debt but individuals in particular should not lose sight of the risks.

Buying something with the help of credit is merely a deferral of payment. You have to find the money sooner or later and, in the meantime, pay for its use. Interest at 10 per cent added each year to a loan of £1,000 nearly doubles the debt to around £1,949 in seven years. Interest rates on commercial loans are invariably more than those offered on deposit accounts; if not, banks and other deposit-takers would soon go out of business.

Few people can afford to buy their first home without a mortgage. All seems sweet and rosy as long as your job is secure and house prices remain steady or are rising. It is not usual for a first-time buyer to raise £125,000 from a combination of personal savings and a loan. A loan of 80 per cent of the value of the property is £100,000 and interest at, say, 6 per cent is itself £6,000 in the first year. The interest and capital repayments can represent a significant proportion of income.

If the value of the house falls by 20 per cent, the buyer's contribution of £25,000 is effectively wiped out, on paper at least. A relatively modest drop in the value of the asset makes a much greater dent in the owner's personal contribution than in the security of a lender (mortgagee). Similarly, if the owner (i.e. mortgagor) loses his job and is unable to match his salary, he may be struggling to meet his mortgage payments. House prices tend to rise in the longer term but there have been periods of significant falls and widespread financial distress.

Before taking on borrowing, it is important to think through the implications and, in particular, the risks of not being able to meet the payments. Unless the interest rate is fixed, factor into your sums the possibility of an increase. Look at the range of products on offer and consider different ways of meeting your aim. For instance, is it wiser to realise a low-yielding investment than to incur the costs of a loan?

If borrowing is the solution, consider how best to formulate and present an attractive application. Put yourself in the position of an objective commercial lender and test your proposition against the criteria he is likely to adopt.

## 5.2 a lender's point of view

Any commercial lender is in business to make a profit. He will assess the risks of a proposition particularly to try and avoid a loss should the borrower default on his payments. If a proposition is acceptable in principle, he will attempt to set an appropriate price through the rate of interest and any other charges. At the same time, he is operating in a highly competitive market so that there are the constraints of market forces on pitching his price too high.

In order to assess an approach, I would expect a diligent lender to seek information on the following.

### purpose

The intended purpose of the facility (i.e. loan or overdraft) is a sound starting point and provides several pointers for assessment of the proposition. In addition, a reputable lender will not wish to be associated with an illegal, immoral or unsocial transaction.

### loan or overdraft

A loan may be needed for the purchase of a specific asset such as a house or a car. The purpose may be less specific, on the other hand, for an overdraft. With an overdraft, the lender allows the customer's current account to go into debit temporarily such as for a few days  in anticipation of his salary. A loan, by contrast, is usually run as an account separate from any current account; the balance of the loan account may be fixed or may fluctuate according to the agreement between the lender and borrower.

### amount

The amount of a facility will be related to other criteria such as the credit standing of the borrower, the means of repayment, the security offered and the time for which it is required. For an overdraft or personal loan, the source of repayment is likely to be future income and the borrower needs to demonstrate the scope for keeping on schedule, taking into account existing debt.

## credit standing, credit scoring

I mean by **credit standing** the reputation of the borrower for discharging his financial obligations. When I was being taught about lending in the late 1960s, the assessment of credit standing was far less structured than it is today. The strength of the connection, the school you had attended, who you knew and how splendid a chap you were carried considerable weight and could tip the scales, even if you were a doubtful proposition by more objective criteria.

**Credit scoring** is now a widespread technique of the major financial institutions. It takes into account all the key criteria and woe betide a lending officer who incurs a bad debt when lending against the advice of a credit score. In addition, there is an ever-increasing exchange of information through the media of credit reference agencies. We are of course talking about a market place that would have been unrecognisable forty years ago and rapid developments in information technology have been both a catalyst and a facilitator of much of the change.

## security

**Security** is usually intended by lenders as a long stop should the primary source of repayment fail. For instance, a house purchase loan secured by a mortgage over the property is serviced out of the income of the borrower. The lender will seek to enforce his security only if the borrower is unable to meet the interest and repayments for whatever reason. A security may, nonetheless, also be the primary source of repayment. Someone buying and selling houses may need a **bridging loan** to match the transactions and the lender will often look to the property being sold as both the means of repayment and as security in the meantime. Lending without security is **unsecured** and poses more risk for a lender.

## guarantee

A **guarantee** is a secondary form of security by which a third person agrees with the lender to meet the obligations of the borrower should the borrower himself fail to do so. For example, a young couple may be able to borrow more to buy a house if a parent enters into a guarantee than they would otherwise. In such a case, a lender will assess the creditworthiness of the guarantor as well as that of the couple and will also take a mortgage over the house as its primary security.

## timescale

The timescale of a facility may be as short as days or weeks – as with many bridging loans – or a period of years. Overdrafts are often in place for year after year but the lender is likely to review them periodically even if the process is merely internal. He may ask questions if the borrowing shows signs of becoming hardcore rather than temporary.

Personal loans for specific consumer goods are often in the region of 2-4 years. Remember that the rates of interest on such loans tend to be high and provide a good incentive to achieve repayment as quickly as possible. Loans for house purchase and improvement may be for 20–25 years although borrowers are developing a tendency to switch lenders if they spot what appears to be a better deal.

## overall proposition

From a lender's point of view, the risks tend to be lower the better the credit standing of the borrower, the more stable the source of repayment, the greater the cover afforded by any security and the shorter the timescale. As noted already, credit scoring is a widely used tool so that credit assessment is becoming more of a science than an art.

## 5.3 sources of finance

Having introduced various dimensions of borrowing, I turn to a brief examination of the principal sources of finance. My first distinction is between private and commercial.

### private

Private sources of finance include parents, grandparents and other relatives who may be prepared to help on a less-than-commercial basis such as by providing an interest-free loan. Ideally, the terms of the loan should be recorded in a simple document, possibly a letter, and signed by all the parties. It is then clear that the transaction is a loan, repayable as such, rather than a gift. If the lender decides to waive repayment at a later date, he should do so by formal waiver whether or not the loan was recorded on paper. Alternatively, he could accept repayment and subsequently pay over the money as a gift with written evidence of his intention.

### commercial

As to commercial lenders, we are talking mainly of banks, building societies, credit card companies, some retailers and finance companies. Banking and lending are, to a point, regulated activities and organisations that conduct them need a licence from the Financial Services Authority. Licensing and regulation are important limbs of consumer protection but are not intended to shield consumers from mere bad bargains. Hence a buyer should still satisfy himself over the terms of a facility, whether or not it is regulated, before committing himself to it.

### house purchase

The major high street banks and building societies dominate the house purchase or mortgage market. Such loans are essentially long term, perhaps 25 years, and the lending is relatively safe in that it is secured and people are reluctant to put their homes at risk. Most mortgages are on a **repayment** basis where part of the monthly payment is applied to interest and the rest to repayment of capital. The monthly payments are designed to clear the debt by the end of the term so that the payments need to be adjusted on changes in interest rates.

An alternative is for the loan itself to remain fixed during its term and for the borrower to pay **interest only** to the lender. At the same time, the borrower enters – or, arguably, should enter – into some sort of savings plan such as an endowment policy that matures in time to repay the loan. The policy (or whatever) is often assigned to the lender as additional security for the loan.[1]

Variations on the theme include **flexible, offset** and **current account** mortgages that are essentially repayment mortgages but allow some flexibility over repayment schedules. With offset mortgages, the facility takes the form of a loan account run in parallel to a current account, whereas a current account mortgage is what it says, an overdrawn current account. The beauty is that interest is calculated on the net balance although the interest rate is normally loaded for the privilege. Such arrangements are particularly suitable for people whose earnings fluctuate widely or who wish to effect repayment as quickly as possible. I provide a summary of some mortgage types in Appendix B.

As well as the major banks and building societies, some specialist lenders offer services to customers who have difficulty in meeting the typical criteria. Such customers are normally seen as high risk, with a corresponding effect on the cost of credit. Mortgage brokers are another line of enquiry, particularly where circumstances are unusual.

The Financial Services Authority now regulates activities of mortgage business and complainants may avail themselves of the Financial Services Ombudsman. Where a firm defaults, consumers have resort to the Financial Services Compensation Scheme. See Section 15.3 for further details.

## consumer goods and services

As for short-to-medium-term facilities, the banks provide overdrafts and personal loans secured or unsecured. Lending by credit card companies is unsecured and generally has the attraction of being interest-free for a few weeks other than for items such as cash withdrawals. Beyond the interest-free periods, the cost of borrowing is expensive as can be the charges for, among other things, failing to make a monthly payment on time.

---

1 A survey commissioned by the Financial Services Authority (FSA), 'Interest-only mortgages – consumer risks [December 2006]', led the FSA to express concerns over interest-only mortgages. The survey revealed that 24 per cent of new mortgages were being taken out on an interest-only basis. The FSA found too that a significant proportion of the borrowers surveyed (up to 15 per cent) had no strategy for repaying their interest-only mortgages and some were unaware of a lender's right to sell the house if they failed to repay the capital.

Store cards are similar in many respects to credit cards except that they are linked to a particular retailer. They may be offered in connection with a discount on the purchase of goods but they tend to be very costly, even by the standards of credit cards, beyond any interest-free period.

Finance companies lend, usually unsecured, for the purchase of particular goods such as cars, white goods and furniture. If you buy, for example, a sofa on deferred payment terms from a high-street store, you probably enter into two contracts, one with the retailer for the supply of goods and the other with a finance company for the credit. Once again, watch the interest rate beyond any interest-free period.

Hire purchase and credit sale agreements are alternative methods to purchase goods with the help of a finance company. However, the ownership of the goods remains with the finance company until all the instalments have been paid and there is then an option to purchase from the finance company. Again, watch the costs. As with house mortgages, there are specialist providers, not least for perceived bad risks.

## Student Loans Company

The Student Loans Company offers loans to students in higher education at favourable rates of interest and on deferred repayment terms. The government has laid down eligibility and other conditions and the Student Loans Company operates the scheme in conjunction with Local Education Authorities. The loans are partly means-tested and partly non-means-tested.

## equity release

House prices have of course risen steadily – and sometimes dramatically – during the last few years and it has had the effect of increasing an owner's **equity** in his property. The equity is broadly the difference between the realisable value of the asset and the total outstanding loans secured on it.

**Equity release** is increasing the borrowing secured on the house either through the first mortgagee (i.e. the existing lender) increasing his facility or by means of the advance of a second mortgage loan by another lender (i.e. second mortgagee). A second mortgagee in particular will look carefully at the current value of the house and factor in a margin for depreciation in value; repayment of his loan ranks after that of the first mortgagee in the event of a sale, forced or otherwise.

A borrower (i.e. mortgagor) may wish to raise finance in this way for a variety of reasons including improvement of his home or substantial repairs to it. He may wish to buy another property in the UK perhaps to let. Another possibility is to finance the purchase of a property abroad. Negotiating a loan secured on the UK house may be more convenient than one in the country of purchase although there is an obvious risk – or possible windfall – with movements in the currency exchange rates.

The purchase of consumer goods and services could supply another motive as might the consolidation of existing consumer debts. The interest rate on a secured loan is usually much lower than on unsecured consumer finance (credit cards, etc.) and may help with earlier repayment of the debt itself.

A few commercial lenders offer **equity release schemes** for elderly people who own their homes, usually free of mortgage, but who are short of income. There are several schemes but they tend to share the characteristics of deferral of interest payments and capital repayment until after the elderly person dies or decides to sell up. The attraction of not having to move is tempered by the ultimate impact of repayment; a serious alternative is to bite the bullet by trading down to a more modest home.

## credit unions

A **credit union** is a community savings and loans co-operative that is owned and controlled by its members. The constitution will include directors and committee members elected in an annual general meeting. Unions may be associated with organisations such as local authorities, trade unions and workplaces. As with banks and building societies, they are regulated by the Financial Services Authority.

The members combine their savings and may obtain loans at relatively low rates of interest. The maximum a member can save with a union is £5,000. The possibility of borrowing in this way is confined to members and criteria will include the ability to repay.

## 5.4  servicing costs

The principal payment for credit is interest, usually expressed as a percentage rate for a year. In addition, lenders may also levy various other charges including an arrangement or commitment fee. Where the borrowing is by mortgage secured on a house, the lender will commission a survey and valuation and recoup the costs from the borrower. There may also be redemption charges, such as for releasing the security, when the loan is repaid. If the loan is repaid before the contractual date, there may be charges for early repayment or redemption.[1]

The rate of interest might be fixed for the duration of the facility or be variable. For relatively short-term personal loans, the rate is often fixed and the monthly payments are a combination of interest on the current balance and repayments of capital. The interest element is highest at the outset and reduces as the capital is repaid.

Variable rates are sometimes expressed as a margin over the Bank of England's base rate, e.g. base + 2½ per cent. Mortgage lenders have their standard lending

---

1 In January 2007, the Financial Services Authority (FSA) expressed concerns to mortgage lenders over the rising mortgage-exit fees they were charging customers on repayment of their loans or on switches to another lender. Broadly, the FSA stipulated that lenders would have to justify fees higher than those originally specified to a borrower.

rates that they gear to the current level of interest rates. Most mortgage lending in Britain is at variable rates although it is sometimes possible to negotiate a rate fixed for a few years at least. A **capped rate** is a variable rate with an upper limit. With variable rates, borrowers are particularly vulnerable to rises in the level of interest rates.

The rate of interest quoted may not be what it seems at first glance. The true rate of interest on a loan repayable by regular instalments can be virtually double the nominal rate. If you borrow £1,000 for one year at 8 per cent calculated on the opening balance, the headline rate ignores the actual rate of interest on the reducing balance. 8 per cent of £1,000 is £80. The average balance for the year is more like £500 and 80/500 is 16 per cent!

### annual percentage rate (APR)

The concept of **annual percentage rate** (APR) is a reasonable tool to compare the overall costs of differing loan packages, particularly where there are charges on top of the normal interest payments. Loan providers have been required to advertise APRs since their introduction by the Consumer Credit Act 1974. The method of calculation has changed over the years but disparities between lenders' practices still exist. As a rule of thumb, however, the lower the APR, the lower the overall cost of the credit.

The principles behind the calculation of an APR are reasonably straight-forward. They recognise that a nominal rate of interest is not necessarily the true cost of borrowing by factoring into the calculation:

- the frequency and timing of the interest payments
- the added costs and fees associated with arranging the finance.

The detailed mathematics are beyond the scope of this book. Borrowers should feel free nonetheless to ask lenders to supply their individual methods of computation.

## 5.5 health warnings

### the small print

When arranging a borrowing facility, look at all relevant factors including the charges and read the small print. The APR figure helps of course with transparency over the costs of borrowing but has its limitations.

At one time, some mortgage lenders insisted on borrowers arranging protection insurance (such as for buildings or accident and sickness) through their own or an associated organisation at less-than-competitive prices. The industry regulators now frown upon such practices but you should still be wary of conditions that may prove expensive or unattractive in another way.

## avoiding unauthorised borrowing

Only borrow through prearranged facilities. If you overdraw your bank account without arrangement or exceed an agreed limit, you can face uncomfortably high interest charges and significant fees for unauthorised borrowing. Similarly, late payment of a loan instalment or minimum amount on a credit card account is liable to hurt your pocket. The moral is to pre-empt such charges rather than try to argue the toss later if you feel hard done by.[1]

## falling into arrears

Should you get into trouble over your repayments, act promptly as the sooner you start to get back on an even keel the easier it will be. Look carefully at how you might rearrange your affairs including the realisation of a suitable asset if you have one available. Can you reduce your outgoings in some way or increase your incomings by working overtime? If all else fails, contact your creditor or seek independent advice before you default on any payments. Your credit rating is at risk if you have a poor repayment record and you loose flexibility if you are in hock to your creditors.

A lender with security is, by and large, in a stronger position than one without. Hence prolonged failure to keep up with your mortgage payments may enable the lender to foreclose on the debt. The result is the loss of your home and an unsecured debt if a forced sale of the property does not cover the outstanding capital and arrears of interest.

Debtors and creditors have various remedies open to them and debtors' options may depend on whether just one debt is at stake or more than one. Credit issues are a specialist area of the law and you should seek advice from an organisation such as a local Citizens Advice Bureau, the National Debtline or a suitable firm of solicitors without delay.

## insolvency

You are insolvent if your debts exceed your assets and you then have the possibility of declaring yourself **bankrupt** or, less drastically, seeking an **Individual Voluntary Arrangement** (IVA) with your creditors. IVAs are a relatively new feature of insolvency law but their popularity is increasingly rapidly. With either bankruptcy or an IVA, you need the services of an authorised **insolvency practitioner** who, like any other professional, will charge a fee.

## 5.6 checklist

I conclude the section with a summary of points to bear in mind.

▸ Try to keep borrowing to a minimum, especially for indulgencies as opposed to necessities.

---

1 As at July 2007, issues had arisen in relation to the level of charges for unauthorised borrowing, and the Office of Fair trading (on behalf of consumers) and eight of the major banks were starting litigation to resolve them.

- Safeguard your credit standing. Simple steps such as making sure you are on the electoral role can help.
- Repay borrowings at commercial rates as soon as practicable. You need some ready money and a reserve for emergencies. Beyond that, remember that the rate of interest on your debt is probably higher than credit interest on a savings account. Even so, weigh up the impact of any early redemption charges against the interest saved by letting the facility run its course.
- Before committing yourself to a facility, consider carefully whether or not you can afford it and how well the costs of repayment will fit in your personal finances. Read and understand the lender's terms and conditions.
- Similarly, evaluate the risks of potential borrowings such as the impact of higher interest rates and the stability of your income. If you are planning to borrow for an investment, e.g. buy-to-let property, be reasonably confident that the returns will cover the cost of finance by a sufficient margin.
- Where practicable and affordable, consider provision for significant risks through insurance. Chapter 6 deals further with insurance.
- Shop around for the best deal and do not be fazed by superficial attractions. Enquire if a lender's mortgage products meet **CAT standards** (see Section 15.3).
- If you encounter problems over repayments or see them coming, tackle them sooner rather than later. Problems of this sort rarely resolve themselves and you can ill afford the extra charges arising from late payments or unauthorised facilities.

# insurance and assurance

introduction – risk – insurance – assurance – design of life policies – annuities – conclusions

## 6.1 introduction

The concept of risk is at the heart of insurance and is the subject if the next section. I turn then to insurance itself and aspects relating to it. Assurance follows and includes the difference between insurance and assurance. Two further sections are devoted to life policies and annuities.

## 6.2 risk

The Little Oxford Dictionary defines 'risk' as the 'chance of injury or loss or bad consequence'. I have seen much more sophisticated definitions but exposure to damage (or injury), loss and harmful outcome (or bad consequence) are always implicit if not explicit.

You can suffer from damage, loss or harmful outcomes in many ways but my primary concern here is with the effect on your personal finances. Emotional, practical, social and other forms of damage can all be significant but are not really topics for a book about personal finance. Nonetheless, someone handling the financial side should, ideally, be sympathetic to non-financial considerations whether they are involved directly or indirectly.

Here are a few examples of events that can lead to damage, loss or harmful outcomes:

- death of a bread-winner or his partner, especially where there are dependent children;
- long-term ill health or a debilitating injury;
- loss of employment or failure of one's business;
- an investment going sour;
- the default of a significant debtor (including a financial institution with which you have deposited money);

- physical damage to, or loss of, property such as houses, furniture and other domestic goods, personal possessions (including jewellery) and cars;
- incurring loss through defective workmanship, professional negligence or fraud by someone else;
- a claim against you for damages;
- the financial collapse of a provider of goods or services, e.g. a travel company;
- the disruption (through bad weather, etc.) of a special event such as a garden fete or wedding;
- the death of, serious illness of or injury to a pet.

If you are aware of such possibilities, you have a choice of providing for the contingency of things going wrong or of leaving matters to chance. The financial consequences of some could be considerable or catastrophic. Take, for example, the death of a bread-winner who is married but whose wife is not working as she wishes to be at home with their young children. The (financial) issues are likely to include the mortgage on the house and an income for the wife and children. Relatively few families have the resources to cope with such disasters unaided.

You can meet some of the above contingencies by taking out insurance. It is difficult or impossible to insure against others, e.g. an investment going sour, but there can other ways to reduce or mitigate the risk. I return the topic in relation to investments in Chapter 8.

## 6.3 insurance

A popular solution to a number of risks is to share the problem with a third party, usually an insurance company or syndicate. Fortunately, many risks are relatively unlikely to happen to most people although they will afflict a few. An insurer calculates through statistics the chances of defined events occurring and offers to provide a specified level of **cover** for payments known as premiums. The premiums reflect, among other things, the claims experience of the insurer, its administrative costs and a profit margin.

### choice of insurer

Broadly, you have a choice between dealing direct with insurance companies and employing the services of an insurance broker. The latter may be particularly useful if the risks (i.e. circumstances) are out of the ordinary or you are having difficulty with finding suitable cover yourself (perhaps owing to a poor claims record). Bear in mind too niche providers, for example ones that specialise in policies for the over-50s.

Your contract may be with a broker – perhaps one operating in the Lloyds of London market – who arranges the insurance itself with underwriters behind the scenes. Price and service levels are important but so is the stability of the insurer and its underwriters. If in doubt, make enquiries about a firm you intend to deal with. A starting point is to ask the firm for information about itself and about its underwriting arrangements.

You do not wish to find yourself without cover because your insurer goes out of business. It would be illegal to continue with pursuits for which insurance is compulsory (e.g. third-party cover for motorists) and unwise in other cases. People with unsatisfied claims may seek help from the Financial Services Compensation Scheme (see Section 15.3).

## insurance policies

The formal contract between the insurer and the customer (the insured) is a **policy** and it sets out the obligations and rights of both parties. Important terms include the events that will trigger a claim and the basis on which the insurer will satisfy it.

For his part, the insured must pay the premiums promptly as well as disclose all material information to which the insurer is entitled both when arranging the policy and while it is in force. Contracts of insurance are ones made in utmost good faith and an insurer may deny its apparent obligations if the insured has failed to disclose something material affecting the risk.

Whether or not you decide to insure against a perceived risk is likely to depend on various factors. You may think the risk too remote and not worth the cost of insurance. You may not be able to afford the premiums, particularly if the insurance fraternity view you as a bad risk, although it may be feasible to arrange some cover albeit not as much as you would like. You may consider that you have resources sufficient to cope should the worst happen; in effect, you choose to self-insure.

## compulsory insurance

At the same time, there are occasions when it is compulsory to have insurance. A notable example is the legal obligation of motorists to insure against **third-party claims**, i.e. claims for injury to others and damage to their vehicles and other property. Such cover is the bare minimum and most drivers should in practice have comprehensive cover that incorporates damage to themselves and their own vehicles regardless of who is to blame.

## protection products

Insurance policies are sometimes termed **protection products** and many cover a range of contingencies. It is not usually possible to speak of a standard policy as insurers have their variations on a theme but the following are examples of typical policies that are widely available:

> ▸ Household – damage to the buildings; damage to or theft of furniture and other contents; damage to, theft of or loss of personal possessions (e.g. jewellery) whether in the house or elsewhere; certain claims by third parties; the legal expenses of pursuing certain claims against others. There is more on household insurance in Chapter 12.

- Motor – accidental damage or theft and fire damage to your vehicle and its accessories; claims by third parties for death, bodily injury and damage to their vehicles.
- Term insurance – for death before a specified date; the cover may be **level** (e.g. lump sum of £100,000), **decreasing** (such as to match the outstanding capital on a repayment mortgage) or **family income benefit** (to pay an income rather than a lump sum to dependants).
- Critical illness – the equivalent of level term insurance except that the insurer pays out in the event of a serious illness (that is carefully defined) rather than on death.
- Income replacement – provides income while unable to work through sickness or injury (the terms are carefully defined).
- Accident, sickness and unemployment – intended to meet mortgage payments while unable to work (again, the small print is critical); another name for this type of cover is mortgage-payment protection insurance (MPPI).[1]
- Personal accident – scale of payments for death or injury such as loss of sight or limbs arising from an accident; often included as a section of motor and of travel policies.
- Private medical insurance (PMI) – intended to help meet the costs of treatment outside the NHS.
- Travel – in relation to holidays, cover for cancellation, missed departure, medical conditions, death or injury, third-party claims, loss of luggage/money/passport, etc.
- Pet insurance – vets' fees on illness or injury, death (cost to replace), loss by theft or straying, damage to property, third-party claims, etc.

### service agreements and extended warranties

There are also home services agreements, akin to insurance, covering problems with central heating, plumbing, drains and electrics. The agreements provide also for routine servicing and safety checks of central heating boilers, gas fires and other installations.

Similarly, extended warranties on electrical appliances feature an element of insurance in that certain repairs and their costs are catered for should the need arise. Manufacturers' warranties and breakdown cover are equivalents for motorists.

It is for individuals to assess if the costs of these 'contracts' are justified by the risks of things going wrong within the stipulated period. A possible expedient is to concentrate on covering the potential 'losses' that would create the greatest inconvenience or disruption.

### policy wordings and exclusions

Insurance policies tend to be tightly worded and it is important to check that they cover fully the contingencies you wish to provide for. Note particularly the

---

1 In early 2007, the Financial Services Authority took punitive action against leading providers of MPPI over poor selling practices.

exceptions, exclusions and excesses. Where there is an excess, e.g. of £100, the insurer will not pay for claims of a smaller amount and will deduct the amount of the excess from larger claims.

Typical travel policies, for instance, have exclusions for hazardous sports and existing medical conditions and an upper age limit of around sixty-five or seventy. Private medical policies also exclude known existing medical conditions and their premiums are related to age and past medical history. They are both instances of where reading the small print is highly desirable. I return to private medical insurance in Chapter 13.

I have mentioned already the dangers of non-disclosure of material information. Many policy documents incorporate express terms in this respect.

### no claims discounts

Some insurers offer no-claims discounts on their premiums, particularly in respect of motor policies although I have also seen them with household policies. A claim is likely to result in a loss of all or part of the discount on subsequent premiums unless the policy provides otherwise. Remember that the discounts are for no claims and that the question of fault for a claim is a separate matter.

### life and general insurance

A distinction is often made between **life insurance** and **general insurance**. Life insurance is really insurance against death whereas general insurance relates to cover against most other contingencies.

## 6.4  assurance

### insurance and assurance

We touched on life insurance with term insurance, personal accident insurance and travel insurance (where there is often some provision for death as a result of an accident on the holiday). In these cases, the insurer will only be liable to pay out if the death occurs within the terms of the policy. **Life assurance**, by contrast, relates to policies that make a payment regardless of when death occurs. Hence the distinction between life insurance and life assurance is equivalent to that between 'if' and 'when' although the term 'insurance' is frequently used loosely in relation to policies that are strictly ones of assurance.

### 'whole-of-life' endowment

Two important categories of life assurance are **whole-of-life** and **endowment**. As you might expect, whole-of-life policies pay out only when death occurs, whatever the age. With endowment, they mature at a specified age (e.g. 60 years) or on death before then.

Either category might be **without-profits** or **with-profits**. With the former, the sum assured under the policy is a sum fixed at the outset, e.g £100,000. With the latter, there is a guaranteed sum assured but it will be less than the sum assured under a without-profits policy for a given level of premium. On the other hand, the insurer (or assurer) adds bonuses to the sum assured, usually on an annual basis, during the currency of the policy.

Insurers reserve for themselves wide powers to calculate the annual bonuses. The idea, however, is to gear them to the performance of the investments made by an insurer from the premiums paid to it less what it requires to satisfy claims under matured policies, administration costs and other legitimate outgoings. In practice, insurers try to take a long-term view of investment performance and smooth the levels of annual bonuses; in good years they keep something back and in bad years they may dip into reserves.

Annual bonuses, once declared and added to the sum assured, are guaranteed. Hence, if Jack has an endowment policy due to mature at age 60 years for a sum assured of £50,000 that has earned annual bonuses totalling £40,000, the insurer will pay out at least £90,000 when Jack reaches 60 or on his death before then. In addition, the insurer may add at maturity a terminal bonus that is not guaranteed in the meantime. By and large, however, terminal bonuses tend to increase with the longevity of a policy and with the success of the insurer's investment performance. Similar principles apply to whole-of-life with profits policies.

For many years, with-profits endowment policies of one sort or another were a popular means to secure a mortgage. The loan would be **interest only**, rather than **reducing capital**, and the house-owner would also start an endowment policy that was designed to repay the entire loan on maturity. His monthly payments comprised, therefore, interest to the mortgage company and life-assurance premiums on the policy. The sum assured was probably less than the amount of the loan but the profits (i.e. bonuses) were expected to more than make up the difference. In the meantime, the house-owner would maintain term insurance to cover any shortfall should he die prior to maturity.

During the 1990s especially, it became apparent that many endowment policies were likely to fall short of the total sum needed to repay the mortgage. Over-optimistic projections of investment performance had clearly been made and the industry regulators became embroiled in a so-called 'mis-selling' scandal. As a result, with-profits endowment policies have acquired a notoriety that, in my view, is not entirely justified.

As you can see, with-profits life assurance tends to have a high element of investment content and a relatively low one of life insurance. With life insurance and, to an extent without-profits assurance, the opposite is true. Hence, when quoting premiums for a life insurance, an insurer is concerned primarily with factors that influence life expectancy: age, whether male or female, health, occupation, pursuits, whether smoker or non-smoker, etc.

Endowment and whole-of-life policies are essentially long-term commitments. The policyholder's circumstances may change, however, so that he wishes to end the commitment prematurely. In the case of with-profits, he might also take the view that the investment returns (in the form of annual bonuses) are unsatisfactory. He can explore a number of avenues.

### surrender

He can seek to **surrender** the policy to the insurer. This means that he stops paying premiums and takes an immediate, discounted sum for his sum assured and accrued bonuses. It is difficult to generalise on figures but the policy-holder is likely to sustain a significance loss on his investment, especially if the policy has not been in force more than a few years.

### fully paid up

Alternatively, he may ask to make the policy **fully paid up**. In this event, he stops paying premiums and settles for a lower sum assured and accrued bonuses payable on the normal maturity date of the policy.

### sale of endowment policy

A third option is try and sell the policy on the open market. There are dealers that specialise in acquiring 'unwanted' endowment policies. They may continue to pay the premiums and receive the sum assured with annual and terminal bonuses on the normal maturity date.

### other investment vehicles

There are, apart from whole-of-life and endowment policies, other forms of life-assurance policy (including **investment bonds**) that are, to all intents and purposes, collective investments. I look at them further in Chapter 8.

## 6.5  design of life policies

### own life

Life policies may be written or designed in various ways. For example, **own life own benefit** relates to a person arranging a policy based on his life and for the benefit of himself or his estate.

### life of another

By contrast, a **life-of-another policy** is intended for one's own benefit but based on the life of another person. The policy-holder must have an **insurable interest** in the other's life; in other words, he must stand to suffer a financial loss from the other's death. Spouses have unlimited insurable interests in each other's lives. On the other hand, a lender has an insurable interest in the life of a borrower only to the extent of the debt and reasonable interest.

**Joint life policies** are generally written on the lives of two people such as husband and wife. The proceeds may be payable on the first death or the second death. To illustrate the difference, let us assume there is a policy written on the joint lives of husband and wife, Antony and Cleopatra, and Antony dies first. With the former, the proceeds are payable on Anthony's death even though Cleopatra is still living. With the latter, the proceeds are payable on Cleopatra's death.

I should add a qualification with the first-death example. Cleopatra would not, as a rule, be entitled to benefit from the proceeds – regardless of whether or not she was named as beneficiary – if she had 'done' Antony 'in'. The point is based on a rule of law that a felon should not benefit from his (or her) felony. Incidentally, I am not intending to suggest that a famous queen of Egypt married an eminent Roman general whom she then 'bumped off'!

'Second-death' policies in particular can have a part to pay in inheritance tax planning such as where use has been made of the **spouse exemption** and inheritance tax (IHT) is payable on the death of the surviving spouse. There is more on IHT in Chapters 7 and 13.

## own life, benefit of another

A further variation is to write a policy on your own life for the benefit of another. If you continue to pay the premiums, they are gifts because you are passing wealth to someone else. Further, the benefits can be subject to a trust, a topic I deal with in Chapter 10.

## 6.6 annuities

Broadly, an **annuity** provides a guaranteed income for life. A person can buy an annuity from an insurance company for a lump sum; the amount of the annual payments will be related to the life expectancy of the **annuitant** (purchaser) and the prevailing investment conditions (notably interest rates) at the time of purchase.

For example, an 80-year-old may buy an annuity and the insurance company may consider that he has a life expectancy of ten years. The insurance company will be committed, nevertheless, to making the payments for the rest of the annuitant's life whether it is one, ten or thirty years, or whatever. From the point of view of the annuitant, the longer he lives the better the deal.

A specific use of annuities relates to pension plans and schemes. Broadly, the funds accumulated can be used to buy (for a lump sum) a retirement income for the pensioner. The insurance company then takes on the risk of the pensioner living longer than expected, although his early death would work of course in favour of the insurer.

A distinction between an annuity bought by an individual outside a pension arrangement (**purchased life annuity**) and one bought inside (**compulsory**

**purchase annuity**) relates to their treatment for income tax purposes. A proportion of the receipts from purchased life annuities is treated as a return of capital and exempt from Income Tax while the balance is taxed as income of the annuitant. With compulsory purchase annuities, the entire receipts are taxed as income. There is more on the rates of Income Tax in Section 7.2.

## 6.7 conclusions

Insurance, whether life or general, is about sharing risk with an insurer for payments known as premiums. Provided the insurers are sound entities and the benefits of their respective policies are equivalent, you should be looking for the lowest premiums for a given level of cover.

The decision to insure or carry the risk oneself depends largely on the potential consequences of things going wrong and the ability to afford the premiums. Most people choose to insure their homes, their furniture and other chattels and their cars for obvious reasons. Most with dependants should insure their own lives and possibly those of their partners.

With life assurance, there is often a high investment content and criteria other than straight costs come into play. You are looking for good investment returns so that the track records and reputations of would-be insurers call for careful scrutiny.

## 7.1 introduction

You may have heard of the saying attributed to Benjamin Franklin that only two things in life are certain, death and taxes. This chapter is intended as a short introduction to the latter. It is a moot point whether or not taxation is an aspect of personal finance. Whatever the correct answer, it is unrealistic to ignore the effects of taxation on many aspects that are undeniably within its scope.

Few of us want to pay any more tax than we have to. Tax is of course crucial to the governance of the nation and the multitude of services provided by the state. More of an issue is how much tax we should pay. It depends largely on the extent of government spending that runs currently at something like 40 per cent of national income.[1] The scope and effectiveness of government spending, and hence the tax take, are political and economic questions that are, mercifully, outside my remit.

Suffice it to say that tax is a far-reaching concept with ragged edges. There are dozens of taxes; levies such as **National Insurance Contributions** (NICs) are strictly forms of taxation even though the word 'tax' does not appear in their names. By contrast, **tax credits** are negative taxes in that they are a means of distributing social security through the tax system.

Few experts would deny that our tax system is complicated. It has evolved since time immemorial (the Domesday Survey of 1086 was for fiscal purposes) and the frequent piecemeal changes encourage fragmentation. Considerable effort is going into a rewrite of tax legislation in modern English as opposed to

---

1 According to figures published with the budget speech of 21 March 2007, total government spending for 2007/08 was projected at 42.6 per cent of gross domestic product.

the traditional legalese. It helps to a point but does not resolve the underlying complexity of the system.

My aim is to make a few general points on taxation and highlight the main personal taxes you are likely to encounter in connection with personal finance. It is impossible in a few hundred words to give more than a flavour of this vast subject.

The government levies tax through legislation (Acts of Parliament) and supplementary regulations. The high-profile aspects are the budget speeches by the Chancellor of the Exchequer but most of the action is behind the scenes. In other words, the politicians in Parliament write the rules based on government policy. On the other hand, it falls to Her Majesty's Revenue and Customs (HMRC) to administer the bulk of the tax system on a day-to-day basis. HMRC establishes and runs the mechanisms for assessment and collection. A notable exception is council tax which is operated through local authorities.

Tax legislation is interpreted according to the meaning of the words used and not the spirit or intention. If HMRC and a tax-payer disagree over interpretation, they may resort to tribunals known as the General and Special Commissioners with a right of appeal from them to the courts (High Court, Court of Appeal, House of Lords, European Court of Justice). There is no equity or fairness in a taxing statute. If something is caught by the legislation, it is taxed, and the other way round, regardless of the merits of the case.

There is an important distinction between **tax avoidance** and **tax evasion**. The former is legal and the latter is not; an evader (as opposed to avoider) who is found out is liable to financial penalties and, in extreme cases, detention at Her Majesty's pleasure.

Tax avoidance is the (legitimate) arrangement of one's affairs to reduce the amount of tax that would otherwise be payable. A simple example is to invest in an Individual Savings Account (see later) rather than outside one to save tax. An example of tax evasion is to omit deliberately a source of income from one's return. UK residents are liable to UK tax on their worldwide income so that failing to declare interest on a deposit account in Bermuda is evasion. In spite of the distinction, the authorities are taking an increasingly dim view of certain contrived schemes of avoidance and introducing measures to close the loopholes in the legislation.

You may also come across a distinction between **direct** and **indirect** taxation. Direct tax is assessed on you by virtue of your income or other criteria; examples are Income Tax and Capital Gains Tax (CGT). Indirect tax is not assessed on you as such although you bear it for some reason; an example is **Value-Added Tax** (VAT) that businesses (on whom the tax is assessed) recoup through an addition (express or implicit) to the prices of their goods and services.

Who is liable to tax? It depends on the tax but most persons or entities are potentially liable to tax on their income and capital gains: individuals (regardless of age), the owners of unincorporated businesses (sole traders and partnerships), the trustees of trusts, the executors of the estate of a deceased person, companies and associations. Registered charities are exempt from most direct taxes, although there are exceptions.

A number of taxes are collected through **self-assessment**. Such a system was introduced in the 1990s for Income Tax and CGT and, although it has come in for criticism, it is in my opinion a considerable improvement on the previous method. With self-assessment, the onus is on the tax-payer to complete his return and to calculate his own tax liability. Needless to say, there are sanctions for people who do not comply.

Here is a brief outline of some of the taxes you are likely to encounter. I base the rates of tax, allowances, etc for 2007/08 on the information published in connection with the budget speech on 21 March 2007. The Chancellor also indicated changes for subsequent years of assessment and I refer to some in this chapter.

## 7.2 income tax

As the name suggests, Income Tax is a tax on a person's total income and is assessed for fiscal (tax) years that run from 6 April year (n) to 5 April year (n+1). Residents of the UK are liable on their worldwide income while non-residents are liable (to UK tax) on UK-source income.

Certain deductions are allowed from gross income and the net amount is the taxable figure. All individuals are entitled to a personal allowance that, for persons under 65 years, is £5,225 for 2007/08; hence, if a person's income after deductions is £20,000, they are taxed on (£20,000–£5,225) £14,775. An additional personal allowance is available to persons registered as blind with a local authority.

The rates of tax are progressive in that they increase with the size of income. The principal rates for 2007/08 are a lower rate of 10 per cent, a basic rate of 22 per cent and a higher rate of 40 per cent and, in addition, there are special rates for dividends and savings. The various categories of income have to be totted up in a certain order so that an essentially simple calculation gets messy.

*Income tax rates for 2007/08*

| Income band | Dividends | Savings | Other |
| --- | --- | --- | --- |
| £1–£2,230 | 10% | 10% | 10% |
| £2,230–£34,600 | 10% | 20% | 22% |
| Over £34,600 | 32.5% | 40% | 40% |

*Notes:*
1 The income assessable is the gross (pre-tax) figure. If tax has been deducted at source, it has to be added back for assessment purposes. With dividends, a non-refundable credit of one-ninth of the dividend itself is added to give the gross.
2 Dividends are treated as the top slice of income, savings income (e.g. interest on bank deposit and government stocks) as the next slice with other income (e.g. earnings, rents, business profits) as the lowest slice.
3 Where capital gains are assessable (see Section 7.3), they are added on top of dividends, etc.

In his budget speech of 21 March 2007, the Chancellor announced a reduction in the basic rate from 22 per cent to 20 per cent and the abolition of the 10 per cent band for other income for 2009/10. The higher rate tax threshold was to increase to £43,000 by 2009/10.

Married couples and civil partners are treated as separate persons for income tax. This was not always the case for married couples and **independent taxation** was introduced shortly before self-assessment. Nonetheless, there are still some special rules for married couples (and civil partners) that give scope for planning to reduce a couple's overall liability.

Not everyone has to complete a self-assessment return, largely because a lot of income is received net of a provisional deduction of tax that is taken into account for the final liability. For instance, employers have to deduct pay-as-you-earn (PAYE) from the pay of their employees and, in many cases, the provisional deduction pretty well matches the actual liability for the year.

For those who need to complete a return, notably higher-rate tax-payers, they should have their returns for the year ended 5 April (n+1) with HMRC by 31 January (n+2) at the latest. If the return is in by 30 September (n+1), HMRC will calculate the liability on the taxpayer's part if he so wishes. There is a facility for filing tax returns on-line.

HMRC operate a 'process now, check later' system for returns. Obvious errors apart, they accept a return at its face value and calculate the tax accordingly. They then have a year or so in which to make more detailed checks and raise enquiries.

Outstanding tax is collected through the PAYE coding system for smaller amounts and by specific remittances for larger amounts. Payments on account (based on projected figures) for the year ended 5 April (n+1) are due by 31 January (n+1) and 31 July (n+1) with a balancing payment (or refund) due by 31 January (n+2).

There are sanctions for not submitting a return on time. Tax not paid by the due date accrues interest and, in 'bad' cases, penalties may be added. There is an obligation on taxpayers to report material changes to HMRC; for instance, a new source of income may necessitate their starting to complete self-assessment returns. Generally, people who have tax to pay but have not received a return should inform HMRC.

The Chancellor of the Exchequer announced, in his March 2006 budget statement, plans to revise the filing dates under self-assessment. Broadly, the government wants tax returns in sooner. The Chancellor was also looking forward to compulsory filing on-line although a lot of work is needed in technological circles at least before the aspiration could become a reality.

## 7.3 Capital Gains Tax

CGT is the counterpart to income tax in that it is a tax on profits of a capital nature. Hence, if you sell some shares at a profit over your purchase price, you make a **capital gain** that is potentially liable to tax. Oh that life were so simple! There are numerous rules of computation including ones that allow you to deduct specified acquisition and disposal expenses from a **gross gain** to give a taxable **net gain**.

A **disposal** of an asset triggers a charge to the tax. A disposal may be **actual**, e.g. a sale, or **deemed**, e.g. a gift. The proceeds for the purposes of the tax are the actual proceeds in the event of an arm's length bargain or the market value on a gift or on a sale below market value. You can find yourself in the realm of higher mathematics if you make a part disposal, e.g. of 500 shares out of a holding of 1,250. Disposals between spouses and civil partners are exempt but the donee inherits the donor's acquisition cost.

**Chargeable assets** include company shares (whether or not quoted on an exchange), land and buildings (other than a principal private residence) and some chattels (such as valuable works of art). There are exemptions for your main residence (but not holiday homes and investment properties), government and company loan stocks and ordinary household goods and furniture.

A complicated **taper relief** has operated from 6 April 1998 and is intended to reduce the tax the longer you have held an asset. An **indexation allowance** applied before then and was designed to exclude from tax the proportion of gains attributable to the increase in the RPI during the period of ownership. Both taper relief and indexation allowance can figure in the calculation of gains on chargeable assets acquired before 6 April 1998 (e.g. in 1990) and disposed of since (e.g. in 2006).

Further detailed rules permit losses on the disposal of some assets to be offset against gains on others. In addition, individuals have an annual exemption of £9,200 for 2007/08. Beyond that, individuals' (net) gains are taxed at Income Tax rates as though they were the top slice of income (see also Section 7.2).

HMRC administers CGT through the self-assessment system and there is a supplementary form for those it affects.

## 7.4 Corporation Tax

**Corporation Tax** (CT) applies mainly to companies and associations. They pay the tax on their **profits** and capital gains instead of Income Tax and CGT. Profits are broadly the surplus of trading and other income over legitimate expenditures. HMRC collects CT through a system of self-assessment.

## 7.5 Inheritance Tax

Inheritance Tax (IHT) is another name for a combined death duty and gifts tax. When a person dies, his estate (the sum of the value of all his assets less his liabilities and reasonable funeral expenses) is potentially liable to the tax. A legacy to the surviving spouse is exempt from IHT but the assets become part of the spouse's estate. The same applies for a civil partner.

Gifts made during lifetime are generally taxed immediately or escape provided the donor survives for seven years without enjoying a benefit from what he has given away; the treatment depends on the nature of the gift. Where gifts have to be accounted for on death, they are added to the estate for working out the total IHT payable.

There are exemptions for certain gifts and legacies (including ones to a spouse as noted above). Agricultural and business assets may attract favourable reliefs that lead to a complete or partial reduction of IHT.

For deaths during 2006/07, the first £285,000 of an estate (net of exemptions and reliefs) was taxed at 0 per cent and the balance at 40 per cent. Hence tax on an estate of £685,000 (including a house) was:

| | |
|---|---|
| On the first £285,000, tax at 0% | £0 |
| On the remaining £400,000 at 40% | £160,000 |
| Total tax on £685,000 | £160,000 |

The nil rate band is increased to £300,000 for 2007/08 and, in his budget speech of 21 March 2007, the Chancellor announced increases in the nil rate band to £350,000 by 2010.

It may be possible to avoid IHT through use of the exemptions and reliefs, provided steps are taken sufficiently early before death. There is also scope for planning through wills, especially where there are a husband, wife and children. I can best illustrate this by means of an example involving two scenarios. I assume that the husband (H) and wife (W) each own an estate of £685,000 and, for simplicity, that the rates are those for 2006/07 throughout.

## Scenario 1

H dies in March 2007 and leaves by his will everything to W. H's entire estate is exempt because of the spouse exemption and no IHT is payable.

W dies in March 2010 with an estate worth £685,000 + £685,000 = £1,370,000 that she leaves to the children. The IHT comes to:

| | |
|---|---|
| On the first £285,000, tax at 0 per cent | £0 |
| On the remaining £1,085,000 at 40 per cent | £434,000 |
| Total tax on £1,370,000 | £434,000 |

## Scenario 2

H dies in March 2007 and leaves by his will £285,000 to the children and the rest to W. The legacy to the children is taxed at 0% and that to W is exempt. There is no IHT.

W dies in March 2010 with an estate worth £685,000 + £400,000 = £1,085,000 that she leaves to the children. The IHT comes to:

| | |
|---|---|
| On the first £285,000, tax at 0 per cent | £0 |
| On the remaining £800,000 at 40 per cent | £320,000 |
| Total tax on £1,370,000 | £320,000 |

There is a saving of IHT in Scenario 2 of (£434,000–£320,000) £114,000 (i.e. £285,000 at 40 per cent).

Alternatively, H could have left the legacy of £285,000 to the children on **discretionary trusts** from which W could have benefited – from the income in particular – during her widowhood. The trust would have remained outside her estate for IHT purposes. The drafting of a will with discretionary trusts is a job for a specialised draftsman.

A possible way of funding IHT on the surviving spouse's death is through a life assurance policy written in trust for the children. The premiums paid by the parents are gifts but may well be exempt. The trust keeps the proceeds out of the parents' estates.

There is more on IHT in Chapter 13.

## 7.6 National Insurance Contributions (NICs)

NICs are tantamount in some respects to a payroll tax. Both employers and employees have to pay NICs at stipulated rates beyond a threshold of earnings. Self-employed persons are also liable to NICs. NICs are significant in determining entitlement to the state pension.

The rates applicable to employees (Class 1 contributions) for 2007/08 are:

Total weekly earnings:

| | |
|---|---|
| Up to £100 | Nil |
| £100 to £670 | 11 per cent* |
| Over £670 on the excess | 1 per cent |

* the contracted-out rate is 9.4 per cent

Employers pay on weekly earnings over £100 at a rate of 12.8 per cent (or 9.1 per cent if the contracted out rate applies).

In his budget speech of 21 March 2007, the Chancellor announced that the NIC upper earnings limit would be aligned to the Income Tax higher rate tax threshold for 2009/10.

## 7.7 stamp duties

There are various stamp duties including Stamp Duty Land Tax (SDLT) and Stamp Duty Reserve Tax (SDRT).

SDLT is charged on an acquisition of land in the UK and calculated as a percentage of the purchase cost. The rates on most residential property for 2007/08 are:

| | |
|---|---|
| 0 per cent | £0–£125,000 |
| 1 per cent | £125,001–£250,000 |
| 3 per cent | £250,001–£500,000 |
| 4 per cent | Over £500,000 |

The same rates apply to non-residential property and to residential property in 'disadvantaged areas' except that the upper limit for the 0 per cent rate is £150,000. The Chancellor announced in his budget speech on 21 March 2007 significant reliefs available from 1 October 2007 for 'new zero-carbon homes'.

The duty is payable by a purchaser. Note the effect of just falling into the next band; for example, the duty at 1 per cent on £250,000 is £2,500 whereas the duty at 3 per cent on £250,001 is £7,500.

SDRT is chargeable on a purchase of marketable securities. As at April 2007, a purchase of shares quoted on the London Stock Exchange for £5,000 would incur SDRT at 0.5 per cent, i.e. an addition of £25 to the cost.

## 7.8 Council Tax

Local authorities levy Council Tax on households within their area. The amount is based on the value of the property. There is a basic assumption that the household comprises a minimum of two residents so, for single-person households, there is a reduction of 25 per cent.

Liability normally falls on residents who have a proprietory interest. There can, however, be a fallback to non-resident owners. Various exemptions apply to students' accommodation, halls of residence and dwellings occupied by students.

Council Tax benefit is available to households on a low income and is means-tested.

## 7.9 significant tax concessions

From the point of view of personal finance, I highlight the concessions available to **individual savings accounts (ISAs)**, registered pension schemes and charities.

### ISAs

For 2007/08, individuals aged 18 years or over may contribute (i) up to £7,000 to a maxi ISA comprising up to £3,000 in cash and the balance on stocks and shares or (ii) up to £3,000 to a mini cash ISA and up to £4,000 to a mini stocks and shares ISA. Sixteen- and seventeen-year-olds may place up to £3,000 in a mini cash ISA. I deal with ISAs in more detail in Chapter 8 but the income and capital gains arising in an ISA are exempt from Income Tax and CGT. They are, in effect, mini tax havens and designed to encourage people to save. There is no tax relief on the contributions to an ISA.

### pension schemes

In similar vein, the Government is anxious that people save up for retirement and hence there are attractive (i) Income Tax reliefs for contributions by employees and self-employed persons to recognised pension arrangements and (ii) exemptions from Income Tax and CGT for income and capital gains arising in a plan or scheme. Pensions are an important area of personal finance and I devote Chapter 11 to them.

## charities

The Government encourages giving to charity through a number of concessions. Gift aid applies for Income Tax and, if you give £100 to a charity using **gift aid**, the outcome is:

- If you are a basic-rate (22 per cent) taxpayer, it costs you £100.00 and the charity receives a total of £128.21 (£100.00 from you and £28.21 from the Exchequer).
- If you are a higher-rate (40 per cent) taxpayer and report the gift in your tax return, the gift costs you £76.93 (after tax relief) and the charity still benefits to the tune of £128.21.

There are a number of conditions relating to gift aid and the donee charity will usually supply the necessary paperwork. You should also keep a record of such gifts for their inclusion in your tax return. Non-tax-payers should not attempt to use gift aid as they can become liable for the tax the charity is able to recover.

There are also important exemptions from CGT for charitable gifts of chargeable assets and from IHT for gifts made during lifetime or by will.

## 7.10  tax credits

The term 'tax credit' is ambiguous. It can relate to the Income Tax deducted at source from your income that is brought into account for the purposes of your overall liability. There is also a system of tax credits that are essentially social security benefits paid through the tax system; they are the subject of this section. The conditions relating to tax credits are quite complicated and I confine myself to short descriptions.

## child tax credit

**Child tax credit** is designed to support families with children and its amount is related to family income and the number of children; broadly, the lower the income and the greater the number of children, the higher the benefit. It is claimable for children up to 16 and, for those in full-time education, up to 18. It supplements any child benefit and working tax credit.

## working tax credit

**Working tax credit** is payable to individuals in low-paid jobs and to working households in which an individual has a severe disability. There are various scenarios in which the benefit may be claimed but, generally, an individual has to be aged 16 or over and live in the UK.

### HMRC helpline

HMRC has a special helpline for those who wish to enquire about the tax credits.

### pension credits

Pension credits are social security benefits rather than tax credits and are operated by the Pensions Service of the Department of Work and Pensions. I look at them in Chapter 13.

## 7.11 suggestions

To round off this chapter, here are a few suggestions.

- Familiarise yourself with the relevant principles of taxes that affect you. Note the use of the term 'principles'; the small print can be daunting but it is easier to tackle if you understand the gist of what the provisions intend. There are several digestible guidebooks available in leading bookshops, particularly ones published by leading newspapers, and the HMRC website contains a wealth of information in relation to Income Tax, CGT, IHT, NICs and stamp duties.
- If you are married or have entered into a civil partnership, do not overlook the possibility of saving tax by reorganising matters between you and your spouse or partner.
- Be meticulous in your record-keeping; you have a statutory duty in this respect and I recommend retaining material information for at least six complete tax years (although, legally, you can often get away with less). I am reiterating here comments in Section 1.2.
- If you need to complete a self-assessment return, make sure you have all the relevant forms (including supplementary sheets for the return itself) and supporting information in good time.
- Complete your return accurately and submit it well before the deadline. If possible, get your return in by 30 September and ask HMRC to work out the tax. Check the figures when you receive them and do not delay in following up any queries.
- Consider the tax implications of any significant actions you propose with your personal finances or of any change in circumstances.

# making your money work

introduction – management – the importance of sound management – basic concepts – collective investment schemes – tax-free wrappers – methods of managing investments – investment policy – summary

## 8.1 introduction

The aim of this chapter is to present a framework for undertaking effective management of your savings and investments. I defined various terms, including 'money', 'savings' and 'investment', in Chapter 2 and I use 'money' in this chapter in a broad sense that embraces savings and investments as well as currency and bank deposits.

Whatever the amount involved – £1,000, £1,000,000 or more – there will be the need for decisions and paperwork. I expressed views in Chapter 1 on developing competence in personal finance and having a sense of purpose and I regard those attributes as essential for the effective handling of significant amounts of money.

I should emphasise that my following remarks are no more than guidelines for application to the particular circumstances of individuals. I do not offer specific investment advice and I am not authorised by the industry regulator to do so. The scope of the subject is enormous and I can do little more than scratch the surface. Even so, this is the longest chapter of the book and I have tried to break it down into manageable chunks.

I start with a definition of **management** and then restate the importance of the sound management of savings and investments. Explanation of some basic concepts follows before an examination of forms of collective investment scheme that can be useful to most investors but especially so where relatively small sums are involved. So-called tax-free wrappers warrant a section to themselves before I round off with remarks on methods of management and on investment policies.

## 8.2 management

In Chapter 2, I treated savings as money put aside for spending in the future. Investment was spending money on an asset with a view to a profit such as a regular return of income. The distinction between the two may be obvious or subtle but the principles of management are similar.

As to management itself, dictionary definitions point to it being in charge of, or exercising control over, something. I advocated in Chapter 1 the wisdom of being master of your own destiny and implementing sound management is an important means to that end. I now draw a distinction between two levels of management. At the higher level, it is about setting direction and making strategic decisions. At the lower one, it is to do with day-to-day administration and making tactical decisions.

Setting direction translates into being clear over your aims and objectives and the general thrust of your policy. You can then fit into that framework decisions over what to acquire, when to dispose of it, how and when to reorganise or improve and so on. They are the key decisions that require long-term and short-term perspectives, particularly the former.

Administration is essentially the task of keeping the show on the road. It involves record-keeping, arrangements for collecting income, the mechanics for dealing with maintenance and outgoings, information for tax purposes, the safe-keeping of documents of ownership and much else. They are arguably the more mundane tasks but failure to keep on top of them is a recipe for chaos. Again, long-term and short-term perspectives are appropriate but with more emphasis on the latter in this case.

## 8.3 the importance of sound management

I can best demonstrate the need for effective management, supported by systematic processes, by giving examples in relation to specific classes of asset. The analysis is to illustrate my point and does not cover everything.

| Asset class | Direction | Administration |
|---|---|---|
| Bank and building society deposit accounts | Term of deposit<br>Rate of interest<br>Level of risk<br>Choice of bank or building society<br>When to encash/switch | Opening of the account<br>Arranging passwords, etc.<br>Obtaining statements, etc.<br>Application of interest (e.g. add to account)<br>Details for tax return |
| Company shares and loan stocks quoted on a stock exchange | What to buy<br>Timing of purchases and sales<br>Exercising rights as stockholder | Safe-keeping of certificates, etc.<br>Arranging deals<br>Receipt of income<br>Details for tax return |

| Property (residential, commercial) | What to buy | Safe-keeping of title deeds |
| --- | --- | --- |
| | Timing of purchases and sales | Collection of rent |
| | Letting to tenants | Repairs and insurance |
| | Rent reviews | Physical inspections and surveys |
| | Improvements and renovations | Compiling information for tax returns |
| | Finance | |

There is a lot to learn if you are starting from scratch but there is some excellent material around if you are prepared to devote time and effort to it. Property law and practice in particular can be highly technical and it will be difficult to avoid the expense of professional charges for some tasks. Section 15.6, supported by Further reading and resources, is devoted to sources of information.

## 8.4 basic concepts

It is worth drawing together a few key concepts that underlie the deployment of your money in savings and investments. I have touched on some in a different context already.

### risk

Chapter 6 on insurance and assurance contains remarks on risk including a dictionary definition of risk as the 'chance of injury or loss or bad consequence'. The definition is equally valid in relation to savings and investment.

Any deployment of money in this way carries some form of risk. The prospect of reward needs, therefore, to be balanced against the risks of what you intend to acquire. Investments that are perceived to be risky need to hold the prospect of sufficiently high rewards to persuade people to take the risks. It follows that patently 'safe' investments such as National Savings products offer a relatively low, guaranteed rate of interest; a speculative investment such as shares in an unproven oil exploration company could prove highly profitable if it struck rich but a disaster otherwise.

Here are some examples of risks attached to specific classes of asset. Again, the analysis is merely to illustrate a point and is not exhaustive. These risks need to be weighed against the potential rewards.

| Asset class | Risks |
| --- | --- |
| Bank or building society deposit | Default of the deposit-taker |
| | Rate of interest becomes uncompetitive |
| | Loss of purchasing power through general price inflation |

| Quoted loan stocks (interest rate fixed) | Default of the borrower<br>Reduction in creditworthiness of the borrower<br>Increase in general level of interest rates<br>Loss of purchasing power through general price inflation |
| --- | --- |
| Quoted company shares | Company does not perform as well as expected<br>Inadequate management<br>Adverse stock-market sentiment (e.g. through decline in the economy) |
| Property (residential, commercial) | Physical damage<br>Problems with tenants<br>A decline in the desirability of the locality<br>Adverse changes in the economy<br>Changes in the demand for particular types of property<br>High costs of acquisition and disposal |

### diversification

A generally accepted method of spreading risk is **diversification**, in other words, resorting to several different investments or not putting all your eggs in one basket. There are various angles to diversifying such as between asset classes and within asset classes.

If part of your money is on bank deposits and part in company shares, you are spreading it between two asset classes. Within bank deposits, you may have a number of accounts with different organisations rather than just one account. Some accounts may be **term deposits** where the interest rate is fixed for a year or more. Others may be **instant-access deposits** where the interest rate is liable to fluctuate up or down. By having these different accounts, you are not eliminating the risks of default of a deposit-taker and uncompetitive interest rates but you are hedging your bets.

Within the class of company shares, there are numerous industry sectors and, within the sectors, several individual companies, although some sectors are much bigger than others and companies vary considerably in size (see also Section 9.3 and Appendix D). Some sectors are regarded as defensive and tend to hold their own even when the general economy is sluggish; food-retailing is one example. Others thrive better when the economy is buoyant; building and construction are examples. If you like banks, there is good reason to have shares in more than one. There are differences between their businesses and the quality of management is an important ingredient for success. Unfortunately, judging how well a company is run can be difficult in the short term at least.

Part of the skill of investment is understanding and interpreting correctly the trends in the economy and how they are likely to affect the level of interest rates, the fortunes of companies and the valuation of property assets. It is not sufficient, however, to study the British economy alone. Britain is part of the world economy and what goes on in the USA, Europe, the Far East, etc. has an impact on domestic fortunes.

The concept of diversification is reasonably straightforward. What proportions should be devoted to specific asset classes and, within those classes, to individual assets is another story and there is no easy answer. A lot depends on what you are trying to achieve and the level of risk you are prepared to accept.

## personal objectives

Investment policy is a very personal affair and has to be related to what an individual wishes to achieve and how. Absolutely right or wrong solutions are rare, although some are clearly more appropriate than others.

Under modern regulation, the first duty of an investment adviser is to undertake a **know-your-customer** assessment. This is a structured fact-find comprising questions to obtain among other things information on the material financial and family circumstances of the customer, what he is trying to achieve, timescales, his attitude to risk and other considerations that may affect a choice of investments. As to the last point, someone vigorously opposed to alcohol and tobacco may stipulate no investment in breweries and cigarette manufacturers.

The answers should guide the adviser towards agreeing with the customer his aims and objectives and how he is prepared to set about achieving them. The process provides a sound foundation for devising an investment policy framework for the selection of specific investments. For someone intent on 'do it yourself', there is every merit in going through a similar process to avoid too many tangents.

## suitability

Another imperative of financial regulation is that advisers should only make recommendations that are suitable, i.e. meet the customer's needs. A number of possible solutions may be suitable and consistent with the customer's aims. On the other hand, a purchase of company shares with a sum of money that is liable to be required at short notice is patently unsuitable; the money should be kept on a bank or building society deposit until it is needed.

Depending on the amount involved, suitable recommendations will involve a degree of diversity in order to spread risk. Most people should retain some money that is readily accessible for unforeseen needs and a bank deposit is an obvious solution. Beyond that, however, a longer-term view may be appropriate and, if it is five to ten years or more, most people should consider company shares through either direct or indirect purchase. I return to the subject later in the chapter.

Suitability can depend on a variety of factors, including an investor's objectives and tolerance of risk. His personal tax position can also have a material bearing.

## income tax

I refer you also to Section 7.2. Interest on deposit accounts and government and other loan stocks is taxed as unearned or investment income of the holder. The payer often has to deduct tax (at 20 per cent in 2007/08) and account for it to HMRC.[1] The holder is assessed via his tax return or through **PAYE**. If he has suffered too much tax, he can get some or all back and, if he has suffered too little, he has to pay the balance.

With gross interest of £100 paid after deduction of tax, the holder actually receives £80 (£100 – £20). If he is not liable to tax, he can reclaim the £20 from HMRC. If his personal rate is 40 per cent, he has to pay a further £20 (directly or indirectly) to HMRC.

Dividends on shares are also taxed as income of the holder. A UK dividend is deemed to carry a tax credit of 10 per cent for 2007/08. Hence a dividend receipt of £90 carries a tax credit of £10 and is regarded as a gross (or pre-tax) dividend of £100. If the holder is not liable to tax, he can no longer recover the tax credit (as he could until a few years ago). If he is a higher rate taxpayer, he is liable to further tax that amounts to 25 per cent of £90, i.e. £22.50, making an total rate of 32.5 per cent on the gross of £100.

## capital gains tax (CGT)

I refer you also to Section 7.3. Company shares are **chargeable** assets for CGT purposes so that gains on disposals are potentially liable to tax. The method of calculating a gain on a disposal or part disposal can enter the realm of higher mathematics. Conversely, losses on sales may be offset against gains realised on other chargeable assets of the taxpayer.

Most government and other loan stocks are not chargeable assets for CGT. This means that gains are outside the scope of the tax and losses cannot be deducted from gains on chargeable assets.

## review

The above concepts are limbs of a systematic process to come up with a coherent plan for looking after one's money. Circumstances may change, however, and it is good practice to review your arrangements from time to time. It is particularly important to review your entire strategy if something unforeseen happens, such as the loss of a well-paid job or a windfall as in the case of an unexpected inheritance.

Even without a change of this nature, it is wise to check the tiller every six to twelve months if only to satisfy yourself that your strategy is still valid and that you are making good progress in achieving your aims. The exercise should include a review of your investments to assess:

- how they have performed (collectively and individually);
- the adequacy of the level of income they are producing.

---

1 With British Government securities, the interest is generally paid gross unless the holder requests that tax be deducted.

It is not unusual for one investment in a portfolio to grow more spectacularly than the others so that the holding becomes disproportionately large. The investment may retain its merits but, on grounds of prudent diversification, consideration should be given to trimming it and to buying alternatives with the proceeds. This is an example of **portfolio rebalancing** and is an important feature of the review process.

## 8.5 collective investment schemes

A particular problem for investors of limited means is obtaining a sufficient diversification of their assets in order to spread the risks of things going wrong. It is true of company shares and it is truer still of property assets where the scope to buy an entire investment property is absent for most individuals.

Others know, for instance, that they want a stake in company shares or commercial property but have little knowledge of what to select and how to manage a portfolio of investments. They are prepared nonetheless to pay a reasonable charge for a professional to perform the management for them. This is where collective investments come in.

The essence of a **collective investment scheme** is that investors pool their resources in an entity that holds and manages assets on their behalf. The entity is run by professionals who understandably are paid for their services through charges levied on the assets and income of the entity. The entity itself owns and runs a portfolio of investments and the subscribers to the entity own shares or units in it. The subscribers have an indirect interest in the underlying assets but it is the entity that owns them directly.

If the entity has a portfolio valued at £20 million and there are 10 million shares or units in existence, the value of an individual share or unit is likely to be in the region of £2. An investor with 1,000 shares or units will have a stake worth some £2,000. If the shares or units were bought for less, the investor is showing a profit and the reverse is true if the shares were bought for more.

The main advantages of investing in this way are a greater range of assets than would be available by investing directly, the professional expertise of the management and the reduced administration compared with direct ownership of investments. Against this, there are the disadvantages of the managers' costs and the dependency on the managers to perform.

There are different types of entity in respect of the way they are constituted and in respect of the investment themes they adopt. There are three main categories, 'approved' investment trusts, 'authorised' unit trusts and 'authorised' open-ended investment companies (OEICs). The terms authorised and approved appear in the tax legislation and my comments do not extend to the unapproved and unauthorised alternatives.

### investment trusts

**Investment trusts** are companies, overseen by a board of directors accountable to the shareholders (i.e. investors), whose business it is to hold and manage investments. The term trusts is a bit misleading in that, legally, these entities are not trusts at all but companies set up and operated under company law. The company itself (i.e. the investment trust) owns a portfolio of shares and the investors own shares in the company. The investment trust shares are quoted on a stock exchange and can be traded (i.e. bought and sold) accordingly.

Investment trusts are said to be **closed-ended** because, by and large, the number of shares in the company stays constant. The value of the shares tends to fluctuate in line with the value of the underlying portfolio of the company. Nevertheless, there is usually a disparity between the price of the investment trust shares and their **net asset value**. The net asset value is, broadly, a proportionate part of the underlying portfolio less liabilities of the company. Investment trust shares tend to stand at a discount to the net asset value but, occasionally, the shares of some trusts rise to a premium.

The board of directors is responsible for making arrangements for the day-to-day management of the investment portfolio. The board has to set strategy, however, and monitors the performance of the investment managers. It may employ its own investment managers or, as is more usual nowadays, delegate the management to a separate organisation.

### unit trusts

**Unit trusts** are in fact trusts rather than companies. They are constituted under trust law, overseen by trustees and heavily regulated under the Financial Services legislation. They are said to be **open-ended** because new units are created or existing units are cancelled according to the demand from investors. Hence the size of a trust varies both with the number of units in existence and with the price fluctuations of the assets in the underlying portfolio.

Unlike investment trusts, the price of the units is directly related to the net asset value of the trust. The method of calculating unit prices is subject to strict rules made by the industry regulators and there may be separate prices for buying and selling.

The promoters of unit trusts generally manage the portfolios themselves and the role of the trustee is akin to that of a watchdog. Among other things, the trustees hold or control the assets held in a trust's own portfolio and they are accountable primarily to the unit-holders (i.e. investors) rather than the managers. It is a regulatory requirement that trustees be independent of the managers.

### OEICs

**OEICs** combine features of investment trusts and unit trusts and are something of a hybrid. They are companies rather than trusts but operate in ways similar to unit trusts; in particular, they are open-ended. For most investors, the technical distinctions between unit trusts and OEICs can largely be ignored whereas those between investment trusts, on the one hand, and unit trusts and OEICs, on the other, can be material. Independent custodians, rather than trustees, look after the interests of the shareholders of OEICs.

## other collective schemes

Other collective schemes include endowment funds and unit-linked products from life-assurance companies, policies from friendly societies, venture capital trusts (VCTs) and exchange-traded funds (ETFs).

As to life-assurance-company products, I commented on endowment policies in Section 6.4. **Unit-linked policies** (or **investment bonds**) are more similar on the face of it to unit trusts and OEICs in that there is a direct link between the performance of the underlying fund and the policy-holder's stake. The life-assurance element of investment bonds is small. An important difference between investment bonds, on the one hand, and unit trusts and OEICs, on the other, is the method of taxation that benefits some taxpayers but penalises others. I describe the tax differences later.

ETFs are a form of **tracker funds** (see below). Their shares are quoted on a stock market and, because of the way in which they operate, their prices and their net asset values are closely related.

## tracker funds

Tracker funds are a growing body of collective schemes that replicate particular stock-market indices. For instance, the FT compiles a number of indices of the London and other major stock markets. The so-called **Financial Times Stock Exchange 100 index** (**FTSE 100**) is made up of the top 100 companies by total market capitalisation (value) quoted on the London Stock Exchange and changes in the index reflect the overall movement of those shares in a trading session. A tracker fund that tracks the FTSE 100 invests in the companies comprised in the index or at least a large representative sample.

There are also funds that track the more broadly based **FTSE all-share index** (which represents over six hundred stocks traded in London) as well as other major indices of the world stock markets. There is a diverse range of ETFs quoted on the London Stock Exchange.

There is no investment management as such and a computer program generates changes in the portfolio of the tracker fund such as when companies drop out of the index and are replaced by others. Tracker funds are said to be passively managed and hence are relatively inexpensive to run by comparison with actively managed funds. Their charges are usually lower with a corresponding benefit to their returns.

## charges

A point to watch with all collective schemes, and particularly unit trusts and OEICs, is the management charges levied against the funds. With unit trusts and OEICs, there is generally an initial charge payable on purchase and an annual charge. Typical charges are 5 per cent or more upfront and 1–1½ per cent annually according to the nature of the fund. You should expect lower charges for tracker funds, ideally no initial charge and ½ per cent or less annually. Look also at **total expense ratios** (TERs) as they reflect all the running costs and not just the manager's own charges; they are frequently in the region of 1.75 per cent–2 per cent on actively managed funds. TERs do not include the direct costs of buying and selling investments.

It may be possible to avoid all or part of the initial charge especially by buying through a **discount broker** or **funds supermarket**. Initial charges are designed, among other things, to provide commissions to introducers of business and some firms are willing to share the benefits to attract custom where they do not offer advice.

## published information

Investment trusts are quoted on the London Stock Exchange and, as public limited companies, have to conform to the normal rules of corporate governance. Their obligations include the publication of annual reports and accounts for shareholders in either a **full form** or a **summary form**. These documents contain important information on the content of the underlying investment portfolio, performance over the period of account, the directors and investment managers and the running costs of the company (including the remuneration of the investment managers and directors).

Unit trusts and OEICs are also subject to strict governance. Their managers publish reports and accounts to meet criteria specified by the rules of the industry regulator, the Financial Services Authority.

It is wise to keep an eye on performance tables although, to paraphrase the words of the regulator, 'past performance is no guarantee of the future'. Even so, there are collectives that have put in consistently good performances and others that have consistently poor records. I recommend taking a reasonably long-term view – of five, ten or even more years – rather than a relatively short one of a few months or a year or two. Various reputable journals and websites compile and publish perfomance tables on a regular basis (see also Section 15.6 and Further reading and resources).

## volatility

The more volatile the performance – i.e. the greater and the more frequent the price swings – the longer-term view you generally need to take of an investment. You should give yourself plenty of room for manoeuvre and avoid being in the position of having to realise an equity-based investment in a hurry. The volatility may mean that the money you had hoped would be there, or was there some time ago, has dissipated with the changing fortunes of the market.

Remember that a 25 per cent drop in an investment that started at £100 results in capital of £75. On the other hand, you need to see a recovery of 33⅓ per cent to get back to £100.

Investment trust shares can be particularly volatile for technical reasons. The disparity (referred to above) between (i) the price of an investment trust share and (ii) its net asset value can widen and narrow quite dramatically and magnify any losses or gains. Gearing (which I explain below) may also exaggerate price fluctuations.

## taxation

It helps to bear in mind that there are two dimensions to consider: (i) the collectives themselves (whether they are investment trusts, unit trusts or OEICs) and (ii) their shareholders or unit-holders. The policy of the tax rules is to recognise that a collective is a sort of intermediary acting on behalf of its investors and, provided its profits are taxed in the hands of the investors, the collective itself should not incur tax or, if it does, it should pass it on to its investors as a tax credit.

There are wrinkles in the policy I have described but we need not concern ourselves with them here. Suffice it to add that approved and authorised collectives have to pay out the bulk or all of their annual income profits that then become taxable in the hands of their shareholders.

Broadly, investors are taxed on (i) dividends on authorised investment trust shares and (ii) distributions on units in authorised unit trusts and OEICs as if their receipts were company dividends (see Section 8.4). Exceptionally, the receipts are taxed as interest where a unit trust or OEIC invests predominantly in government or other loan stocks.

Capital gains realised by investment trusts, unit trusts and OEICs on their underlying investments are exempt from CGT. On the other hand, the investors' shares or units are chargeable assets for CGT purposes (see also the subsection on CGT in Section 8.4) subject to an exemption for unit trusts and OEICs that invest predominantly in government and other loan stocks. Hence a sale or other disposal by an investor may give rise to a liability to CGT.

The tax treatment of an insurance company investment bond is rather different. The insurance company itself has had to pay Corporation Tax on the income and capital gains of its managed fund. As a result, basic-rate taxpayers do not pay further tax on their profits (whether derived from income or capital) but non-taxpayers cannot recover tax paid by the insurance company.

For higher-rate taxpayers, the arithmetic is intricate but the principles are:

- On maturity of the bond, the gain is potentially liable to Income Tax (but not CGT as a rule).
- Interim withdrawals are tax-free if they do not exceed 5 per cent a year of the sum invested; the annual allowances are cumulative; withdrawals that exceed the accumulated allowances may incur tax.
- Interim withdrawals are taken into account in the calculation of the gain on maturity.
- To the extent that higher-rate tax applies, the rate (for 2007/08) is 40 per cent less a notional credit of 20 per cent for tax incurred in the bond resulting in 20 per cent.

- Divide the gain on maturity by the life of the bond (in years); treat the resulting figure as the top slice of the holder's income for the year; calculate the average rate of tax on the top slice.

*Example*
Gain £20,000; life of the bond 10 years; top slice £20,000/10 = £2,000
Average rate of tax is less than 20 per cent if part only of the top slice incurs higher rate tax (i.e. the other income is below the higher-rate tax threshold)

- Apply the average rate of tax (on the top slice) to the entire gain.

## real-estate investment trusts

A few unit trusts specialise in commercial property (retail, offices and industrial) and enjoy favourable tax treatment on their income and capital gains.[1] Property investment companies, on the other hand, can suffer from an element of double taxation in that they pay Corporation Tax on their profits while their shareholders pay income tax on their dividends and CGT on disposals of their shares.

From 1 January 2007, property companies can become **real-estate investment trusts (REITs)** provided, among other things, they meet certain conditions with regard to the nature of their assets and are prepared to distribute 90 per cent of their profits on their rental business to the shareholders. REITs are not liable to Corporation Tax on their rental profits so more will be available for their shareholders. The shareholders will be taxed on the profits so distributed as if it were rental income in their hands. In addition, there is a generous exemption from tax on capital gains arising from the disposal of assets used in the REIT business.

Given the nature of commercial property, the concept of REITs strikes me as sound but the proof of the pudding will be in the eating. Property investment funds (PIFs) is another name for REITs.

## choosing a collective

As a rule of thumb, the safest choice of collective investments for most private investors is unit trusts or OEICs. Some investment trusts have performed well over the years but tend to be more risky because of the absence of a direct link between share prices and net asset values and because also of **gearing**. Gearing is another name for borrowing. Unlike unit trusts and OEICs, investment trusts can borrow to increase their portfolios and, while it is advantageous when share prices are rising, it works in the opposite direction when they are falling.

As noted, the taxation of life-assurance company bonds differs from that of other collectives, and potential investors need to consider carefully suitability to their particular circumstances. Remember that the tax on income and capital gains within a bond is not recoverable by a bondholder. It means, for instance,

---

1 Nonetheless, authorised unit trusts incur Corporation Tax on their rental income. In March 2007 the Government announced plans to afford property unit trusts a broadly similar tax framework to REITs.

that a holder cannot use his annual CGT exemption to shelter capital gains realised within the bond. By contrast, other forms of collective are exempt from tax on capital gains within the entity; unlike investment bonds, shares or units in the collective are chargeable assets but gains qualify for the annual exemption.

Certain friendly-society policies are exempt from tax but their premiums are limited to £270 a year. VCTs attract major tax concessions but are too risky for many people to entertain seriously.

As to investment themes, investment trusts, unit trusts and OEICs all cover a wide spectrum. There are many generalist funds that offer a broad spread of investments:

▸ company shares
▸ fixed-interest securities
▸ all the major industry sectors
▸ all the major geographical areas (the UK, the USA, Europe, Japan, Far East, emerging markets, etc).

Others specialise such as by:

▸ geography (the UK, the USA, etc.),
▸ sector or theme (financial, health, mining, private equity, social responsibility, etc.),
▸ size of company
▸ investment style (capital growth, high income, income and growth, etc.).

I have also mentioned tracker funds.

## 8.6 tax-free wrappers

Certain investments are themselves exempt from Income Tax and CGT either wholly or in part. Examples include National Savings Certificates and certain small friendly-society policies referred to above. As noted already, interest on government and other loan stocks is taxable but capital gains are exempt.

Other investments attract exemptions if held in a tax-free wrapper although in practice they may be only partially tax-free. Important ones for individuals are pension contracts and individual savings accounts (ISAs). I devote Chapter 11 to pensions and I deal here with ISAs. A further category is **child trust funds** (**CTFs**) although, as the name suggests, they are available only to children, born from 1 September 2002. Finally, venture capital trusts (VCTs) and **enterprise investment schemes** (**EISs**) are not for the faint-hearted.

### ISAs

As described in Section 7.9, the essence of ISAs is that individuals aged 18 years or over may contribute an annual sum up to a specified amount into a small tax haven. The government's intention is to encourage saving.

The current rules are complex in that there are mini and maxi versions. Broadly, for the tax year 2007/08, (i) up to £3,000 may go on a cash deposit plus up to another £4,000 in stock market investments or (ii) up to £7,000 may go into stock-market investments. Mini cash ISAs are available to 16- and 17-year-olds. The government announced in December 2006 plans to abolish the distinction between mini and maxi ISAs so that there may be contributions of (i) up to £3,000 to a cash ISA and (ii) the balance of an overall limit of £7,000 to a stocks and shares ISA. The proposals are expected to take effect from 2008/09. In his budget speech of 21 March 2007, the Chancellor also announced increases to £3,600 for cash ISAs and to £7,200 for the overall limit from 2008/09.

Interest on deposit accounts and fixed-interest investments is exempt from Income Tax. As explained earlier, income from company shares bears a tax credit of 10 per cent. The credit is not refundable even for ISA holders but higher-rate taxpayers pay no more Income Tax on their dividends or distributions. Capital gains are exempt. The government pledged also in December 2006 to retain the tax benefits of ISAs 'permanently'. Note, however, that contributions to ISAs do not attract tax relief (unlike contributions to pension contracts).

## PEPs and TESSAs

**Personal equity plans** (PEPs) and **tax-exempt special savings accounts** (TESSAs) are predecessors of ISAs but additions to them (other than of accumulated income) are not permitted. Continuing holders retain their tax benefits.

The characteristics of PEPs are similar to those of ISAs but subject to minor differences. The government announced in December 2006 that PEPs would be placed on an identical footing to ISAs except in respect of the ability to make further contributions.

## CTFs

The government makes an initial contribution of £250 (or £500 for parents on a 'low income') and a further sum when the child reaches seven. Parents and others can contribute up to £1,200 a year and the tax treatment of CTFs is equivalent to that for ISAs. A child can only receive his funds at age 18. Clearly, the investment of the funds is long term and needs careful consideration from the outset. The government announced in December 2006 that maturing CTFs could be rolled into ISAs to retain the tax benefits.

## VCTs and EISs

The government tries to encourage investment in fledgling companies through VCTs (collectives) and EISs (generally single companies) by means of attractive income tax and CGT reliefs, subject to strict conditions. Such investments can carry above-average risk by their nature and tend to be of greatest potential benefit to higher-rate taxpayers.

It is nice to have wealth but it can add to your worries. Gaining the full benefit entails effective management and there are various ways in which to achieve it. The broad choices are to 'do it yourself' (DIY), or pay someone else and a mixture of DIY and paying someone else.

### complete DIY

With complete DIY, you initiate and make all the decisions, hold the investments in your own name (solely or jointly with your partner), do all the research and complete all the paperwork. It can be quite onerous and time-consuming depending on what is involved.

### total delegation

With total delegation, your main involvement is to find and appoint an adviser, agree the strategy and review progress periodically (perhaps annually) with your adviser.

Tracking down a suitable adviser needs thorough investigation and personal recommendations can be helpful in making a suitable appointment. Typical candidates include independent financial advisers, banks, accountants and investment managers.

As you are likely to be handing over control of your funds, you should be satisfied about the financial strength of the firm and its arrangements for keeping clients' money separate from the firm's own funds. A **clients' money account** is effectively a trust fund for the firm's customers to ensure that, if the firm goes under financially, its creditors have no recourse to the customers' money. There may also be help from the Financial Services Compensation Scheme if the firm went under (see Section 15.3) but it is strictly the last resort.

The firm will undoubtly wish to hold your investments in its nominee company to avoid involving you in individual transactions and to simplify the administration generally. It will collect and account to you for the income and provide information for your tax return. It may even prepare your tax return as a supplementary service. It will also provide periodic valuations of your investments (probably six-monthly) and report on progress.

A decision over total delegation is a function of the level of service you expect, the charges you are prepared to pay and the amount involved. Many investment management providers will be looking to a minimum of £100,000 and some will only entertain considerably more.

Smaller portfolios will often be invested in a range of collective schemes with different themes. Larger ones may be invested in direct holdings or a combination involving collective schemes for a stake in specialist areas.

### mixture

There are many options over partial delegation but, typically, you can hand over the administration but retain the strategic decision-making. In this case, you entrust the custody of your funds to your adviser but decide yourself what and when to buy or sell.

## savings schemes

Contributing to an investment trust, unit trust or OEIC savings scheme is a form of partial delegation. You may pay, say, £250 a month to the scheme manager who then buys more shares or units in your specified entity. You are often free to contribute more, to cease contributions and to withdraw funds when you like but the plan manager automatically assumes much of the administration. The charges vary from manager to manager.

Investors of lump sums often try to time their purchases to when they think the stock market is low. Timing is notoriously difficult; the market's level at any particular time represents, by definition, a consensus of all investors. Regular savings schemes mean the timing is done for you and they help counteract the general volatility of share prices. In other words, they carry the benefit of **pound cost averaging**. By investing a set sum automatically every month, you acquire more units in a month when the market is low and fewer when it is high.

## 8.8 investment policy

I have already written about personal objectives and being clear about what you want to achieve financially and the degree of risk you are prepared to take. It is on such a basis that you can compile a sensible strategy or policy for acquiring a range of specific investments. Each of these investments should satisfy the test of suitability to your aims and needs.

### liquid reserves

Most people should set aside a sum that is readily accessible for a rainy day. Opinions vary over the amount but suggestions of 3–6 months of normal income or expenditure are common. An obvious home for the reserve is a high-interest deposit account with a leading bank or building society where the money is available by instant access or within a few days.

Similarly, there may be merit in making special provision for known commitments. For instance, if you intend to buy a new car in two years and have some or all of the money already, keeping your money in a deposit account is appropriate. By contrast, if you are saving for educational fees ten or more years hence, it is worth considering longer-term investments such as a collective investment scheme based on stock-market holdings.

### capital growth versus income yield

Although peoples' aims and needs are unique, they tend to translate into one of a few principal options for investment policy. An emphasis on high capital growth with little or no immediate income is at one end of the spectrum while a high immediate income with little or no growth in capital or income is at the other. Between the two extremes, there is some sort of balance between a moderate but rising income on the one hand and a reasonable prospect of capital growth on the other.

## income yield

An important criterion in investment selection is income **yield**. The yield is the annual income produced for each £1 invested expressed as a percentage. For a deposit account, it is broadly the same as the **annual equivalent rate (AER)**. If interest at 4.50 per cent is credited to the account just once a year, the AER is also 4.50 per cent. If interest at 4.41 per cent is credited monthly, the AER is still 4.50 per cent because, after the first month, interest is earned on interest as well as on the initial deposit.

Turning to loan stocks, 4 per cent Treasury 2020 is an imaginary government stock (gilt). The government has to repay the stock in 2020 and, in the meantime, the holder of £100 (nominal) of the stock receives interest (before tax) of £4 a year (payable as £2 half-yearly). The stock is quoted on the London Stock Exchange and its capital value will fluctuate with the general level of interest rates. If rates have risen since the stock was issued, the quotation might be £80 for £100 (nominal) of stock; i.e. it costs you just £80 to buy £100 of stock that produces interest of £4 a year.

The income yield on your purchase is [(£4 income) / (£80 cost) × 100 =] 5 per cent.

A similar calculation applies to company shares, also known as **equities**. ABC plc ordinary £1 shares (the company is fictitious) are quoted on the London Stock Exchange at £3 a share (including, for convenience, stamp duty and transaction costs). The company pays dividends totalling 6p a share annually.

The dividend yield on a purchase of 100 shares is [(100 × £0.06 dividend) / (100 x £3 cost) × 100 =] 2 per cent.

With equities, a low dividend yield is often a characteristic of a company that is perceived to carry high prospects of growth in capital and future income. Conversely, a high yield denotes lower market expectations. Note the term expectations; companies often disappoint the market and their share prices suffer accordingly. The point reinforces the logic of maintaining a range of holdings either directly or indirectly (through a collective investment scheme) to reduce the risk of individual stocks not meeting expectations.

## redemption yield

**Redemption yields** apply to government and other loan stocks with a fixed repayment date. They are not easy to explain but I will make an attempt with an example that oversimplifies the arithmetic.

*Example*

Another (imaginary) government stock 3 per cent Treasury is redeemable on 31 December 2016 and its market price on 31 December 2006 is 88 (i.e. £88 per £100 nominal of stock). Using the income yield calculation above, the stock's **running yield** on 31 December 2006 is:

(£3 income) / (£88 cost) × 100 = 3.41 per cent.

The stock is standing at a discount to its par or repayment value, £88 against £100, so that a current holder who retained the stock to redemption in 2016 would make a guaranteed capital profit of:

(£100 − £88) / 88 × 100 = 13.63 per cent or, broadly, 1.36 per cent p.a. over the ten years.

The redemption yield is the running (income) yield plus the annual capital profit, i.e. 3.41 per cent + 1.36 per cent = 4.77 per cent.

An oversimplification is that I have ignored the time element in respect of the capital profit – 1.36 per cent in year two is worth less than 1.36 per cent in year one, and so on. Also, my calculation shows the gross yield. The net yield would take account of a deduction for Income Tax on the running yield although the capital profit will be exempt from CGT. I hope, nonetheless, that the principle is clear. Appendix C pursues the mathematics.

If you want to compare a 'dated' government or other stock with an alternative investment, it is more meaningful to look at the redemption yield rather than the income yield to match total prospective returns. If a stock is standing above par, i.e. at a price greater than £100 per £100 nominal of stock, the capital element works the other way round, so to speak. In that case, you make a similar calculation but deduct the prospective capital loss from the running yield.

## building a portfolio

I noted in Section 8.4 that all investments carry risks of one sort or another. Investment in equities is often seen as inherently risky by comparison with putting your money on a deposit account or buying government securities. It is true in some respects but investing in companies, directly or indirectly, is one of the few ways in which you can expect to retain the purchasing power of your savings over the longer term. Short-term timing of purchases and sales is another issue and beyond the scope of this book.

Property is another hedge against inflation, although sizeable sums are needed to buy individual properties and they may not be easy to sell at short notice. There are already a few collective schemes for commercial property that help to provide a spread and the benefit of professional management; REITs (described in Section 8.5) add a further dimension. In any event, many people already have a significant proportion of their resources tied up in bricks and mortar in the form of their homes.

The conventional wisdom is to have a decent spread of suitable investments. The precise composition will depend, however, on individual objectives and preferences. A possible expedient for someone who is cautious but would like some spice is a core-satellite policy. The core is a high proportion of the portfolio invested in steady assets. The satellite is a small proportion ring fenced for riskier propositions.

You can achieve such ends through a range of collective schemes. Suitable candidates for the core are generalist schemes, with a wide spread of equities by sector and geographically, and low-cost funds that track the major indices. The satellite might be devoted to more 'exciting' themes such as smaller companies and emerging markets where the prospective rewards are higher but so are the risks.

Tax benefits can often ratchet up the returns but never let the tax tail wag the investment dog. In other words, choose an investment primarily because it is suitable and, if there is a tax benefit available, so much the better.

Holding investments in an ISA wrapper is likely to be attractive for most investors because of the tax advantages, the wide choice available and the flexibility of withdrawal. The tax treatment of pension schemes is, in some respects, even better but there are serious constraints on when and how their benefits can be drawn. I delve more into Pensions in Chapter 11 but, before that, I introduce Wills and trusts in Chapter 10. Meanwhile, Chapter 9 develops the theme of investment.

## 8.9 summary

This is a relatively long chapter and I summarise the themes as follows:

- You should manage your savings and investments.
- I identified two levels of management. The higher level is concerned with strategic direction based on what you are looking to achieve. The lower one is about the detail of day-to-day administration.
- Consideration of risk – what can go wrong – is a necessary discipline. Diversification is an important tool to help manage risk.
- Investments should be suitable to circumstances and needs. Tax considerations are a limb of suitability.
- Collective investments are useful for diversification and professional management but choose wisely and watch the charges.
- Take advantage of tax benefits, such as through ISAs and pension funds, where they benefit your game plan.
- Consider how much you want to take on yourself and delegate the rest to reliable professionals.
- Whatever your level of involvement, you are in charge so review objectives, policy and performance at least annually or on changes in circumstances.

# investment: an art or a science?

introduction – investment versus speculation – an example of investment practice – investing in emotions – is it art or science?

## 9.1 introduction

This chapter is to all intents and purposes an extension of the previous one. The idea is to develop the theme of Section 8.8 by looking further into the nature of investment.

Back in the 1960s, I sat (and passed!) an examination set by the then Institute of Bankers called The Principles and Practice of Investment. I was specialising in the administration of estates and trusts and an important duty of trustees was – and very much still is – the proficient investment of their trust fund. Incidentally, there is more on Wills and trusts in Chapter 10.

One of the topics early in the syllabus was the difference between investment and speculation and then you went on to the principles of investment followed by **practice**. Chapter 8 is concerned mainly with principles so this one focuses more on practice spiced up with a few more principles. A short comparison with speculation comes first.

Practice has to recognise that investment takes place in the real world where it is unusual for anything to be logical and clear-cut. Individuals behave with varying degrees of rationality and, in any case, we all have feelings. Hence I introduce later in the chapter an element of emotional evaluation with the help of a scenario based on circumstances that I have come across in practice. I round off the chapter with an opinion on whether investment is an art or a science.

## 9.2 investment versus speculation

In Chapter 2, I suggested that with investment, money is spent on an asset with a view to a profit such as a regular return of income or a capital gain. For speculation, I have resorted to the Collins English Dictionary (1979 edition) where there are definitions of the verb to **speculate** and the noun **speculation**. I quote both.

There are three limbs for 'to speculate' and they are all helpful:

1 'to conjecture without knowing the complete facts';
2 'to buy or sell securities, property, etc for the hope of deriving capital gains';
3 'to risk loss for the possibility of considerable gain'.

We have for speculation 'investment involving high risk but also the possibility of high profits'. We might add a time perspective in that speculation is often seen as short term whereas investment tends to be regarded more as long term.

As you can see, there is a potential overlap between investment, on the one hand, and speculation on the other. I remember scratching my head in 1967 and trying to fathom out where one ended and the other started.

One of the icons of the investment world was an American called Benjamin Graham who lived from 1894 to 1976. His pupil and disciple Warren Buffett is perhaps better known nowadays and is often referred to as 'the Sage of Omaha'.

Graham wrote a book *The Intelligent Investor: A Book of Practical Counsel* (New York: Harper & Row, 1949), that Warren Buffett has described as 'by far the best book on investing ever written'. Chapter 1 of the book was entitled Investment versus Speculation: Results to Be Expected by the Intelligent Investor. In it, he reproduced a formulation from an earlier book *Security Analysis* (*On the Choice of Investments*) (New York: McGraw-Hill, 1934) he had co-authored with David Dodd just after the Great Crash of 1929–32: 'An investment operation is one which, upon thorough analysis, promises safety of principal and adequate return. Operations not meeting these requirement are speculative.'

The point is the degree of analysis that is put into the selection of the specific share or other proposition. The more information you have or can deduce, the more you can manage the risk and the less the level of conjecture over making a profit or a loss.

For example, a problem with a gold mine is knowing how much of the metal is present in the ground, how accessible it is and the future price of gold. With a supermarket, on the other hand, you can gain a pretty good idea of the value of the company's assets (including its properties), the quality of its management and the trends in its trading performance. Hence a gold mining share may be regarded as more speculative than a supermarket one. Nonetheless you might invest in either on the basis that you have made a detailed study of the information reasonably available to you and have made an informed judgement.

On a more frivolous note, there is an analogy with gambling. If you pick out a horse with a pin, you are clearly speculating. If you study the form of the horse, the trainer, the stables, the jockey, the state of the course, etc and take a more measured view, can you call it investing? It is questionable in that the only asset is your claim against the bookmaker if the horse turns out to be a winner. On the other hand, I have heard it said that people stick pins in newspapers to choose which shares to buy.

## 9.3  an example of investment practice

I use a hypothetical set of circumstances in this section.

### scenario

Juliet is seeking investment advice. She is 52 and was widowed a few months ago when her husband Romeo choked on some spaghetti. She has two sons, Tom (aged 26) and Rick (aged 24), now owns the family home and has £30,000 of her own on bank deposits. Juliet also has £500,000 as a result of Romeo's death that she needs to invest.

Juliet is in good health and intends to leave her estate to Tom and Rick. She receives a modest pension from her late husband's employment and estimates that she needs an income of about £15,000 a year from her investments. She is a basic-rate taxpayer.

Juliet accepts that she has a realistic life expectancy of around thirty years and that a sensible investment strategy is a balance between immediate income and capital growth. She would in fact like to see a steadily rising income for her benefit with long-term growth in the capital for her sons' ultimate benefit. She is willing to accept a moderate level of investment risk to try and keep up with inflation.

During an initial discussion with Juliet, there is broad agreement to retain her bank deposits as a reserve and to invest the £500,000 in a mixture of:

- fixed interest securities confined to gilts and the bonds of blue-chip organisations;
- a range of UK company shares;
- collective investment schemes to provide a stake in overseas markets and other niche areas.

Index-linked gilts are regarded as unattractive at current prices. Collectives might include tracker funds and commercial property funds. National Savings Certificates, particularly the index-linked issues, were considered but rejected as there is no immediate income and they are usually of greater benefit to higher-rate taxpayers than basic-rate ones.

I assume investment conditions similar to those at the end of 2006. For simplicity, I ignore tax by regarding the income figures as gross (i.e. pre-tax), treat incidental purchase costs (including commission) as included in the figures and omit considerations of investment timing. Some of the investments should be wrapped in an ISA for the tax benefits.

Before outlining a specific portfolio, I look at ways of selecting particular stockholdings. I remind you too that the exercise is purely hypothetical and that I am not authorised to offer specific investment advice.

### fixed-interest stocks

I introduced in Section 8.8 the concepts of income yield and redemption yield and illustrated the principles with imaginary government stocks. With the 3 per cent Treasury 2016, the government is due to repay it at par (i.e. £100 cash for £100 nominal of stock) on 31 December 2016. I estimated a redemption yield of 4.8 per cent with the stock standing at 88 on 31 December 2006.

The fact that the stock stands below par means that there is some prospect of capital growth if it is held to redemption as well as a secure annual income in the meantime. Juliet, as a basic-rate taxpayer, will be taxed on her interest but any capital gains on fixed-interest stocks will generally be tax-free.

Partly because of the tax treatment, I am reluctant to invest in stocks standing over par and regard a small range of stocks with varying redemption dates as desirable. They will provide a sound level of income although growth prospects will be limited.

### company (ordinary) shares

I expressed the opinion in Section 4.9 that company share analysis is a complex yet fascinating subject and entails both quantative and qualitative skills. I need to put flesh on the bones.

There are two principal share markets in London, the **main market** and the **Alternative Investment Market** (**AIM**). The requirements for gaining a listing on the main market are more onerous than for AIM and the constituents of AIM tend to be smaller, less mature companies albeit there are notable exceptions. Again for simplicity, I confine myself to main market companies but the principles for AIM companies are broadly similar.

The *Financial Times* newspaper divides the market into sectors and there are varying numbers of company in each sector. I reproduce in Appendix D the *FT* sectors with the number of companies in each. Share prices appear most days in the *FT* and other newspapers, although the others do not necessarily include the prices of all companies or divide them into the same sectors.

A typical approach to analysing a share is to start with an appraisal of its sector by looking at factors such as commercial and economic conditions and prospects for growth. For example, Food and Drug Retailers contains the major (quoted) supermarket chains that compete ferociously. There are, however, high entry barriers for would-be newcomers. The sector is mature although companies such as Tesco are growing through diversification into non-food retail and other activities and expansion abroad.

The next step is to examine individual companies. They are subject to strict rules for reporting profits, balance sheets and other information of interest to investors. The reports and accounts are available from the companies themselves although stockbrokers and others often distribute their own research material, particularly to their clients. In addition to the numbers, it is important to gain a feel for less tangible factors including the quality of management.

### dividend yield, earnings yield, dividend cover, price-earnings ratio

We are now re-entering the realms of percentages and ratios and my mathematically challenged wife has sounded a health warning. If calculations switch you off, do not worry as it is the conclusions that count.

I mentioned dividend yield in Section 8.8. It is a company's annual dividends expressed as a percentage of the share price and varies with dividend changes and price fluctuations.

Similarly, **earnings yield** is a company's earnings per share expressed as a percentage of the share price. **Earnings** are roughly a company's net profit for a year divided by the number of shares in issue.

**Dividend cover** denotes how many times a company's annual profit will pay its dividend for the year. Hence, if the earnings per share are 18p and the dividends total 6p, the cover is three times. If dividend and earnings are equal, the company is paying out its entire net profit. The higher the cover, the safer a dividend tends to be regarded.

The **price-earnings (P/E) ratio** is the earnings yield the other way up and it is this which is usually shown in the *FT* rather than the earnings yield. A share price of £3 and earnings per share of 18p produces a P/E ratio of (300p/18p) 16.7; in other words, it takes 16.7 years to buy the current earnings. The lower the P/E ratio, the cheaper the share – probably a reflection of investors' perceptions of its prospects.

For Juliet, I am looking at a mix of:

- well-established companies with a reasonable dividend yield (over 3 per cent), healthy dividend cover ($2^1/_2$ times or more) and a likely P/E ratio of 10–15.
- less mature companies with greater prospects of growth; I anticipate a dividend yield of less than 2 per cent and a P/E ratio of over 15.

I have included in Appendix D columns for dividend yield, dividend cover and P/E ratio.

### collectives

Section 8.5 deals with collective investment schemes and, in this case, you are looking mainly at the focus of a scheme, the quality of the investment management (based partly on the track record) and the running costs. You are not so concerned with the individual companies in which the scheme invests because that is the role of the manager.

Prices of collectives are shown in the *Financial Times* and other daily newspapers. Investment trusts appear under the investment Companies sector of the *FT*'s 'London Share Service' and most unit trusts and OEICs under the 'Managed Funds Service'. Where separate buying and selling prices are shown for managed funds, you acquire them at the higher one and dispose of them at the lower one. Prices are also available from the managers and often appear on their websites.

For Juliet, collectives are useful to help diversification into more specialist areas such as overseas markets (the USA, Europe, Japan, Asia, etc.) with possibly a small stake in emerging markets. There are the choices of specific country or area funds (e.g. ABC European Fund) and more general international funds (e.g. XYZ International Growth Fund), although the latter may include some UK companies. Collectives are also a way of stretching to commercial property.

For smaller portfolios (a few hundred thousand pounds or less), many wealth managers now prefer the use of in-house collectives to direct investment in specific company shares for even the core content. I have sympathy with this trend provided the performance is up to scratch.

## Juliet's portfolio

I now pull together the theory by suggesting a type of portfolio that might be suitable for Juliet. There is always room for opinion in tasks of this sort and I am concerned to create a flavour rather than a strong taste.

| Content (and objective) | Value £ | Income yield % | Income p.a. £ |
|---|---|---|---|
| Bank deposits (reserve) | 30,000 | 4.50 | 1,350 |
| Fixed interest (secure income and some capital growth) | 125,000 | 4.00 | 5,000 |
| UK companies – mature, bias to defensives (steadily rising income and modest capital growth; indirect international exposure) | 200,000 | 3.25 | 6,500 |
| UK companies – growth (low initial income but good prospects of capital growth) | 50,000 | 1.75 | 875 |
| Collectives (growth from overseas markets and smaller companies; stake in commercial property) | 125,000 | 1.25 | 1,562 |
| Totals | 530,000 | | 15,287 |

Variations on the theme include:

- Part of the £500,000 could be retained on bank deposit. This could be particularly relevant for the proportion earmarked for fixed interest if a rise in interest rates seemed more likely than a fall (higher rates tend to depress fixed-interest stock prices).
- Even if Juliet is not earning, she has scope to pay into a stakeholder pension scheme to build up a deferred income (see Section 11.4).

Building the portfolio is just an initial step. It is important that it continues to be managed even if reasonable professional charges are at stake.

## 9.4 investing in emotions

Investing is commonly seen as a rational, intellectual pursuit rather than an affair of the heart. It is true to a point but, with some so-called investments, there is a significant element driven by the emotions that should be recognised as such. The criteria for comparing predominantly financial investments and ones that tug at the heartstrings are different and the point of this section is to examine a possible approach to a proposition that combines the two elements.

I class as purely financial investments the likes of bank and building society deposit accounts, government and company loan stocks, company shares, commercial property funds and other collective investment schemes based on marketable assets. They can carry an emotional element but potentially more emotional investments include paintings, wine, stamps, vintage cars, antiques and other memorabilia.

Individual properties, particularly first and second homes, fall somewhere between the two extremes. You need somehow to assess such hybrid investments from the distinct points of view of (i) financial worth and (ii) emotional (i.e. enjoyment) value before attempting to reconcile the two results.

This section is perhaps something of a diversion or indulgence and there are not necessarily any right or wrong decisions. I am seeking to put forward arguments that might help someone in a dilemma of this sort arrive at a sensible conclusion of his or her own.

### scenario

A married couple, Jack and Jill, have accumulated a sum of £40,000 that they wish to set aside for future enjoyment. They regard it as a nest egg on which they can draw for holidays and other leisure pursuits.

Jack and Jill are in their late forties and their children are independent of them. They have a reasonable level of earnings from their employments but limited capital apart from their house in suburban Kent valued at £250,000. They have paid off their mortgage and would like to move to a more rural location. They are tied to suburbia by their jobs for the foreseeable future, however, while the cost of houses in the areas to which they are attracted is prohibitive. They enjoy visiting rural England but would also like to take more holidays in other parts of the world. They estimate that the overseas holidays which interest them cost about £1,000 a week each, i.e. a total of £4,000 for a fortnight.

### options

They start by considering several modes of investment but whittle it down to a short list of three.

*Option 1*: place the money on an Internet bank account that would currently yield 5.25 per cent gross or 4.2 per cent after tax of 20 per cent. The starting post-tax income would be 4.2 per cent x £40,000, i.e. £1,680 a year, but the rate of interest would be liable to fluctuate up or down with the general level of interest rates. The monetary value of the capital would remain stable although the balance of capital and hence the income earned would reduce as a result of expenditure.

*Option 2*: buy units in an equity income fund with an income yield of 3 per cent gross or 2.7 per cent after dividend tax of 10 per cent. The starting income would be 2.7 per cent x £40,000, i.e. £1,080 a year, but hopefully the rate of income distributions would increase steadily. The capital value would be liable to fluctuate but they consider that the balance of the investment should grow at 4 per cent a year on average over the next ten years. This represents a total return of 6.7 per cent (2.7 per cent + 4.0 per cent) ignoring any liability to CGT.

*Option 3*: buy a small house in a market town about 120 miles north of Kent at a total cost (including stamp duty and professional charges) of £160,000. They would need to borrow £120,000 – secured probably on their Kent house – at a starting annual percentage rate of 5.5 per cent. They would want to use the house themselves at weekends and for occasional holidays and offer the use of it to relatives and friends. They estimate annual costs of:

| | |
|---|---|
| Mortgage interest (5.5 per cent x £120,000) | £6,600 |
| Heat, light, water, Council Tax, insurance, maintenance, etc | £2,400 |
| Travel to the house and back | £2,000 |
| Total | £11,000 |

In addition, they would forgo the income return they could earn on alternative investments.

They have sufficient earnings to meet the outgoings and they recognise that interest rates may rise, thus increasing their outgoings. They cannot predict the future trend in house prices but would look to capital appreciation to compensate for the costs of upkeep and provide them with a profit. There is of course the possibility that the house would fall in value, especially in the short term.

Their next step is to evaluate the options in relation to financial worth and emotional worth.

## evaluation – financial worth

*Option 1*: this is arguably the least risky in investment terms. Their balance of capital would retain its monetary value and, with luck, the interest would at least match the rate of inflation. The £40,000 represents in effect ten annual holidays at a cost of £4,000 each in current prices and, depending on the timing of the holidays, there might be some interest left over for trips within England.

*Option 2*: this carries, on the face of it, more risk, particularly in the short term, but a greater potential reward. They might get ten holidays costing £4,000 but they might also get fewer or more, depending on the performance of their investment.

A variation on Options 1 and 2 is to put some of the money – say half – on deposit and the rest in the equity income fund to hedge their bets. Commentators recommend taking a five-year view at least on equity investments, so splitting the money 50/50 and using the deposit account first would give the fund a few years in which to perform. With both options, there is unlikely to be much of the original £40,000 left over once they have had their fling. They would, however, have saved the annual outgoings on the property: £11,000 p.a. for 10 years is £110,000 without adding anything for interest

*Option 3*: this carries far more risk on paper than Options 1 and 2. If interest rates rise, their outgoings will increase correspondingly and there is no guarantee that capital appreciation will outweigh the regular outgoings. The total estimated annual outgoings of £11,000 represent 6.9 per cent of the cost of the house (£160,000) so the house would need to appreciate at 7 per cent a year or more on average for them to break even. The £11,000 is also equivalent to 27.5 per cent of their starting capital (£40,000).

Other financial factors to consider:

▸ The fact that the property would be unoccupied for significant periods is a risk and there are also the logistics of maintenance. Letting it to generate an income is, on the face of it, impracticable and would carry further risks.
▸ Changes to legislation, e.g. a hike in Council Tax, could have an impact on their outgoings and hence the rate of return needed to break even.
▸ As a second home is involved, CGT stands to dilute their return should they realise a substantial profit.
▸ It would probably be cheaper to stay in a B&B than buy a house for visits to their favoured area.
▸ They are dependent on their earnings to meet the outgoings on the house. How secure are their jobs and what would they do if one or both were out of work?

## evaluation - emotional worth

The financial evaluation is largely about figures whereas the emotional one is predominantly qualitative and more subjective.

Options 1 and 2 should take care of holidays abroad for a period of ten years or so. Jack and Jill could of course forgo some of those trips and either save the money or use it for other things such as trips within England. With both options, emotional risks include (i) not going on as many holidays as they had planned and (ii) the holidays they decide to take not coming up to expectations.

Option 3 provides for weekends away from Kent but nothing in the foreseeable future for overseas trips. If in time they make a financial killing on the house, the profit might fund foreign holidays in years to come although it might be necessary to sell the house to release the cash. The satisfaction of owning another house – which could arguably come under the category of consumer goods in these circumstances – has to be weighed against the anxieties of ownership.

Another possibility is that Jack and Jill may find jobs in the locality of their second home that would enable them to sell the house in Kent to pay off the loan and release money for other purposes. It could also be a fallback if one or both were made redundant.

## conclusions

The figures provide a good indication of what is and is not possible in terms of finance. They also point to the monetary risks and rewards. It is for Jack and Jill, on the other hand, to decide their priorities with regard to the use of their money, having regard to (i) the emotional satisfactions they value most highly and (ii) the consequences for their material wealth now and in the future. The primary decision lies with the emotions of the heart but with due regard for the rational calculations of the head.

## 9.5  is it art or science?

The easy answer is to say that investment is a mixture of art and science. I argue, however, that it is one rather than the other.

Several years ago, I read a fascinating article in a weekend newspaper about an old lady who had made a fortune on the stock market. She had started off with a small legacy from her father and the value of her shares had grown well into seven figures. When asked how she had done it, she responded to the effect that she had kept her eyes open. If, for instance, she went in a store and was impressed by what she saw, she bought some shares (provided of course that they were quoted).

I have a high regard for intellectual skills such as law, accountancy and number-crunching in general. I admire enterpreneurial skills even more – an ingenious idea (the simpler the better), the recognition of a commercial opportunity, the confidence in one's own ability, the determination to see it through.

Intellectual skills are not necessarily science but I regard those that I have described as being more science than art. Entrepreneurial skills are not exactly art but I see them as more art than science; there is a heavy reliance on intuition although it is often supported by rational thought and sound judgement.

I think the little old lady was an entrepreneur but was she a speculator rather than an investor? How well had she done her analysis to limit the risk? It is difficult to say. She was not, on the face of it, into figures but they can often be misleading, especially if relied upon slavishly. She conducted her research by keeping her eyes open and her wits about her and, let's face it, her technique did the trick.

I suggest that she was an investor and that investment is primarily an art. Science is useful if you undertake it thoroughly and apply your findings wisely. What really counts, however, is the entrepreneurial flair that the lady in the newspaper demonstrated so well.

wills and trusts

introduction – trusts – wills – acting as executor or trustee – summary

## 10.1  introduction

As with taxation, it is debatable if wills and trusts are topics of personal finance. I have decided to include this chapter, however, as they are closely related to the topic even if they are not strictly part of it.

I start with trusts. The concept of a trust is not always easy to grasp and is still unknown in some systems of law. Trusts are important nonetheless in many aspects of English law, not least in relation to pension schemes that figure in Chapter 11. The development of trusts can be traced back to medieval times so they are not new! Wills follow trusts. A further section on 'Acting as executor or trustee' recognises that taking on the administration of a will or a trust warrants careful consideration.

## 10.2  trusts

The essence of a trust is an arrangement under which trustees look after money (in a broad sense) for others. Trust law defines how trusts are started, operated and ended; the duties and rights of trustees; the rights and duties of the people (beneficiaries) for whom the trustees operate the trust.

Once a person (known as the **settlor**) has placed money (in whatever form) into his trust, he ceases to own it or have any control over it unless the terms of the trust state otherwise. It is possible for a settlor to appoint himself as a trustee or to name himself as a beneficiary.

A specific example of a trust may help in understanding what they are all about.

Jim and his wife Gladys are in their 70s. They are wealthy and wish to give £250,000 to their grandchildren Anna (aged 4), George (aged 2) and any further children of their son Tom and his wife Louise. They would like to make the gift as soon as possible with a view to saving Inheritance Tax when they die.

Anna and George are too young to handle signficant amounts of money until they are at least eighteen and Tom and Louise may have more children who stand to benefit. One solution is for Jim and Gladys to create a **settlement**, i.e. a type of trust fund, for their grandchildren.

Jim and Gladys need to enter into a formal document (a **trust deed**) to start the settlement, to specify the terms and conditions on which the funds are to be held and to appoint trustees to carry out their wishes. They ask Tom and his brother Bill to be the trustees and they agree to this.

The deed specifies that Jim and Gladys will transfer cash of £100,000 and investments valued at £150,000 to Tom and Bill. Following the transfer, Tom and Bill are responsible for the management of the trust fund in accordance with the provisions of the trust deed. The principal terms include the following:

1 Tom and Bill will manage the cash and investments transferred to them and whatever assets they hold for the time being;
2 The beneficiaries are to become entitled to their respective proportions of the capital at age 25. Between 18 and 25, they are entitled to a share of the income. Until then, the income is to be added to the capital.[1]

An initial task for Tom and Bill is the suitable investment of the cash contribution of £100,000. They can employ and pay professional investment managers to run the entire portfolio although Tom and Bill remain responsible for setting the investment policy. They must also review periodically the performance of the portfolio and whether or not to continue with the services of their chosen investment manager.

Note the distinction between **legal interests** and **equitable interests**. The trustees are the legal owners in the sense that they control the assets held in the trust fund; unless delegated, they make the decisions to buy and sell, collect the income and various other tasks. The beneficiaries are the equitable owners which means that they are entitled eventually to the financial benefit of the trust fund; they can enforce their rights against the trustees should the need arise. Beneficiaries have no direct control, however, over the individual trust assets before (in this example) they reach the age of 25.

This is a typical example of a **family trust** or **private trust**. There are, in practice, many variations on the theme. Trusts are generally appropriate to look after wealth for people who are incapable of doing so for themselves. The incapacity may arise for a legal reason, e.g. being under 18 or mentally disabled, or for practical reasons such as irresponsibility with money or

---

1 This type of settlement was popular until March 2006 as it qualified as an 'Accumulations and Maintenance Trust' for Inheritance Tax. The Chancellor announced in his 2006 budget speech the withdrawal of many of the reliefs and the government passed the legislation in the Finance Act 2006. Settlements in this precise form are likely to be less popular in future.

insolvency. Trusts may help also with arrangements to reduce inheritance and other taxes.

An example of a **corporate trust** is a **company pension fund**. The purpose of the company pension fund is to secure the retirement benefits (mainly pensions) of the members (the company's employees and former employees) and trustees are appointed to look after their interests.

## 10.3 wills

Wills can serve several purposes the most notable of which is to enable the maker of the will (the **testator** or, if female, **testatrix**) to specify what is to happen to his **estate** (his **assets**), after satisfaction of his liabilities, following his death.

It is not obligatory to make a will and, generally, only persons over 18 have the capacity to do so. In the absence of a valid will, a person is said to die **intestate**. Who benefits from his estate is then governed by statutory rules of distribution. The intestacy rules prefer close relatives such as spouse and issue (children, grandchildren, etc) to more distant ones.

Any adult with significant assets, including a house, should at least consider whether or not to make a will. Houses and other assets held jointly often (but not always) pass directly to the a surviving joint owner regardless of the terms of the deceased owner's will. On the other hand, a surviving spouse does not necessarily benefit from the entire estate of the dead partner in the absence of a will.

As well as dealing with the entitlement to a person's estate, a will enables a testator to:

▸ appoint suitable executors to administer his estate;
▸ appoint guardians of his minor children (if any at the time of his death).

The role of an executor is a responsible one and can be onerous. You can nominate a lay person, a professional (such as a solicitor), a bank or a combination (up to a total of four). Professionals will expect to be paid for their services (i.e. when they administer the estate after the testator's death) and you should obtain their agreement or that of a layperson before completing the will.

An executor starts his duties once the testator has died. An immediate task is to arrange the funeral or at least check that it has been organised. The other main duties are: to prepare a list of all the testator's assets and liabilities and to value them; to apply to the probate registry for formal authority to administer the estate; to assess and pay any Inheritance Tax (i.e. death duty); to collect in and, as far as it is necessary, realise the assets; to pay the debts and any other liabilities of the deceased and the estate; to pay fixed-sum legacies (e.g. 'the sum of £5,000 to my friend Albert'); to distribute what remains of the estate (the residue). You can create a trust by will and the trustees may be the same as the executors or they may be different people.

A person with overseas assets, especially a house or apartment, should consider a separate will made under the laws of the place where the property is situated. The laws of other countries, particularly in continental Europe, can be different to ours.

In England, testators are relatively free to leave their estates to whomsoever they wish. There is not complete freedom, however, in that disappointed spouses and other 'dependants' may have a legally enforceable claim for due provision.

The formalities for drawing up a will by most people are very strict and date back in some instances to the Wills Act 1837. Broadly, they require a written document, the signature of the testator and the involvement of two independent witnesses. In addition, the testator must have sufficient mental capacity and not be subjected to undue influence or coercion. Writing a will may not be as easy as it first appears and employing a professional (such as a solicitor) may save considerable trouble and expense later on.

For wealthier testators, a will may provide an opportunity to save Inheritance Tax (outlined in Section 7.5). Professional advice is generally wise in such cases.

Wills and trusts are highly technical and the above remarks provide little more than a flavour. Pensions are another potential headache and I tackle them in the next chapter. Before that, I sound a few cautions about taking on the role of trustee or executor.

## 10.4 acting as executor or trustee

Imagine you are having tea with your aunt Gertie in her front room. You do not see her often as you live two hundred miles away but like to call when you can.

Gertie is in her late 70s, has never married and lives alone. She had always lived with her older sister Dolly until Dolly died a few years ago. The house had been Dolly's but, under her will, she left it in trust so that Gertie had the use of it for her remaining years. The trustees are one of your cousins and a local solicitor.

Gertie turns the conversation to her own will. She wishes to make a new one in which she benefits her twelve nephews and nieces (of which you are one). It is a dialogue you would have preferred to avoid but you make some general suggestions for which Gertie is grateful.

Gertie then asks you whether you will be an executor along with her solicitor. After some momentary apprehension, you express your delight in being asked to do so comforted by the thought that she is a sprightly old thing, her estate should be reasonably straightforward to administer and the solicitor can do most of the work.

A few months later, Gertie dies suddenly and, sure enough, she has completed a new will with you as an executor. You have an initial meeting with your co-executor on the day of the funeral and all seems sweet and rosy. The solicitor will do the most of the donkey-work although you will take responsibility for sorting out the chattels.

It is soon realised, however, that there is a complication over Dolly's will trust. The clause in the will dealing with the house after Gertie's death is badly drafted and you find yourself in a squabble between some of the nephews and nieces over who should benefit. Gertie's estate is, according to one interpretation, a potential beneficiary of the proceeds of the sale of the house so that you, as an executor of Gertie, as well as one of her beneficiaries, are in an awkward position.

Matters rumble on and litigation is narrowly avoided. Six years later, you are able to call it a day and bundle up the pile of correspondence files.

Believe it or not, it is a true story, with the identities disguised and with me as 'you'. My aunt knew that I was experienced in estate and trust administration and, with hindsight, I suspect that the wily old bird had concerns over her late sister's will.

The moral of the story is not to take on the responsibilities of executor or trustee without being reasonably confident that you can cope. It involves a familiarity both with the rights and duties of the office-holder and with the circumstances of the particular case.

There are several good textbooks on the roles of executors and trustees but they are not exactly light reading (see Further reading and resources). The best I can do here is to give a taste of the topic. For convenience, I term executors and trustees as fiduciaries, and trust or estate as an entity.

The overriding duties of fiduciaries are (i) to administer their entity according to its terms and the law generally and (ii) to treat their beneficiaries fairly, particularly where there are beneficiaries with competing interests. In addition, there are numerous, more specific requirements, a selection of which I describe briefly.

- Fiduciaries must keep the assets of their entity separate from their own and from those of other entities of which they are a fiduciary. This means, among other things, separate bank accounts that should normally be operated by all the fiduciaries if more than one is appointed.
- Fiduciaries must keep comprehensive records and be able to produce accounts of their transactions.
- Fiduciaries are personally liable for the commitments they enter into on behalf of the entity. They may recover from the entity expenditure incurred for legitimate purposes and in good faith.
- Fiduciaries should avoid conflicts of interest between their entity and their personal affairs. For example, they may not buy an asset from, or sell an asset to, their entity.
- Fiduciaries are under well-established duties of care to their entity and its beneficiaries and they may be personally liable for losses incurred if they have not been diligent. The duties apply among other things to them investing suitably the assets of the entity and keeping the portfolio under review.
- Fiduciaries have powers to delegate certain functions (including the

management of investments) to appropriate agents and to take advice from solicitors and others. Nonetheless, fiduciaries are primarily responsible if things go wrong although they may have recourse to an agent whose performance has not come up to scratch.

- There are strict rules on what remuneration and expenses may be paid to a fiduciary out of the entity. Lay fiduciaries are entitled to reimbursement of out-of-pocket expenses only, unless the will or trust instrument provides otherwise.

I could go on but I hope the above list gives a sufficient flavour. I am not saying that you should never act as a fiduciary and there may be occasions on which it is entirely appropriate that you should do so. The important things are to know what you are doing, to take account of the risks that are entailed and when to take professional advice.

## 10.5 summary

- Trusts are entities, managed by trustees, that serve purposes such as:
  - safeguarding money for people who are unable or unwilling to manage it effectively themselves;
  - conferring limited or successive interests, e.g. 'to pay the income to my wife/widow during her life [i.e. limited interest] and, on her death, to divide the capital between my children' [a trust of this sort might well appear in a will].
- A will directs who is to benefit from a person's estate on his death. Adults should at least consider the need for a will and not assume that the intestacy laws are an appropriate substitute. A testator can create trusts by his will and needs to do so for minor beneficiaries. A testator can also appoint testamentary guardians of his minor children. An executor (appointed by will) is responsible for administering the estate after the testator's death.
- The roles of trustee and executor are responsible ones and can expose the office-holders to personal liabilities. If asked to act as one, you should have a reasonable idea of what is involved before accepting the appointment.

pensions

## 11.1 introduction

For the purposes of this book, a pension is an income in retirement. This simple definition masks, however, a mind-boggling web of issues that embraces the disciplines of politics, economics, law and taxation to mention but a few. My aim is to examine the bones of the subject and to skate round most of the technical complexity.

Most (but by no means all) people aspire to a time when they can cast off the pressures of work and concentrate on the things that they really want to do. As a general rule, they need a reasonable level of income to see them through their remaining years. A typical method of provision is through a pension built up during their working lives.

A pension is not the only way of securing an income in retirement. Some self-employed people and the owners of family companies retain a stake in the business and continue to draw an income by one means or another. Alternatively, they may sell the concern and live off the proceeds. Others are fortunate enough to inherit wealth that produces an income sufficient for their needs.

Relatively few employees are able to accumulate sufficient capital from their own savings to assure a comfortable retirement and have to look to their earning power for future as well as current income. The same is true of many self-employed people who may cultivate a successful business but need something more for continuing financial health.

In broad terms, pensions may be provided in three ways:

1 by the state and financed through National Insurance Contributions levied on employers, employees and self-employed people;

2  by an occupational scheme sponsored by an employer although employees generally (but not always) contribute as well as the employer;
3  by a personal plan maintained by an employee or a self-employed person although, in the case of employees, employers may also contribute.

Leaving state pensions aside for the moment, the government encourages private pension provision through attractive tax concessions. Private in this context takes in occupational schemes and personal plans; occupational schemes apply to public-sector as well as private-sector employees. In order to qualify for the tax privileges, schemes must be registered with HMRC or, prior to 6 April 2006, be approved by HMRC.

Contributions are deductible, within limits, from income or profits assessable to tax. Further tax reliefs enhance the returns on the investments held within the schemes or plans. Much of their income is exempt from tax although dividends suffer a rate of 10 per cent that is not recoverable. Capital gains are also exempt.

On the other hand, benefits paid in the form of pensions are taxable in the hands of the recipient and occupational schemes have to operate PAYE for their members as employers do for their employees. Funds withdrawn in other ways often suffer tax too.

I return now to the three categories of pensions I identified above.

## 11.2  the state pension scheme

The state pension scheme has two tiers, a flat-rate basic pension and the earnings-related state second pension (S2P). A person's entitlement is generally dependent on his record of NICs and the basic pension is reduced if there are insufficient contributions reckoned by years of a deemed working life. S2P is calculated by contributions on earnings between upper and lower limits and is built up accordingly. Only employees have access to S2P; people who are self-employed do not.

Men become entitled to their pension at age 65. The age for women has been 60 but will increase to 65 by 2020.

Certain partners (including married women, widows and widowers) can qualify for state pension by virtue of their partners' qualifying years and earnings. People over 80 not already in receipt of the basic pension may qualify on a non-contributory basis provided they meet certain residence qualifications.

It is possible to **contract out** of S2P by equivalent provision through a private scheme as a result of which employers and employees pay reduced NICs. The arguments over whether or not to contract out can be highly technical and are beyond the scope of this book.

Pensioners on low incomes may supplement their incomes by claiming pension credit. There are two credits, a guarantee credit for people over 60 and a savings credit for those over 65 who have a modest income in addition to their pension.

I look at the amount of the state pension and pension credits in Section 13.3. However, the state pension alone is not likely to meet the aspirations of many people for a comfortable income in retirement. Hence successive governments have sought to encourage further provision through private schemes.

The state scheme operates on an **unfunded** or **pay-as-you-go** basis. Current NICs are used to pay the pensions of retired people.

## 11.3 occupational schemes

Occupational schemes are ones involving an employer. There are different types of scheme and I need to define a few terms.

Entitlement to a pension and other benefits is part of the contract between employer and employee. Promises of pension are often secured by the establishment of a pension fund into which the employer and, if the scheme is **contributory**, employees pay contributions. The pension fund is in fact a trust fund and a panel of trustees, generally comprising representatives of employer and employees, is appointed to administer it according to a trust deed and the rules of the scheme.

The amounts of contributions, usually a percentage of salaries, are calculated by **actuaries** (statisticians of sorts) and varied from time to time to meet a number of criteria. Pension schemes secured in this way are **funded**. Occupational schemes generally have provision for employees to make **additional voluntary contributions** (AVCs) beyond the contractual norm; such a facility may well appeal to **late entrants** who lack pension entitlements from previous employments.

Funded schemes may be **insured** or **self-administered**. With the former, the trustees hold an insurance policy or group of policies and pay the insurance company to provide the benefits and undertake much of the day-to-day management and administration. With the latter, the trustees are directly responsible for payment of the benefits and for most of the functions of management and administration; in practice, they delegate specified tasks to investment managers, actuaries, lawyers and other professionals.

The pension schemes of civil servants and some other public-sector employees are unfunded. There are no pension funds as such and pensions in payment are met, in part at least, out of the current contributions of employers and employees. Government bodies are the employers and national revenues underwrite the schemes. The actuarial (statistical) value of pension promises in the public sector tots up to many hundreds of billions of pounds that are 'off balance sheet'.

With funded schemes, there is a further important distinction between **final-salary** (or **defined-benefits**) schemes and **money-purchase** (or **defined-contributions**) schemes.

With a final-salary scheme, a member's pension is calculated by a formula that incorporates his salary in a period leading to his retirement date. A **sixtieths scheme** is broadly one-sixtieth of final salary for each year of service.

The maximum pension of a sixtieths final-salary scheme is typically 40/60ths, i.e. two-thirds, based on 40 (or more) years of service. A retiring employee usually has an option to exchange part of his pension for an immediate **lump sum**. **Eightieths schemes** with a maximum pension of 40/80ths, i.e. one-half, of final salary are also common. Incidentally, a scheme that provides 40/80ths plus a (tax-free) lump sum of 1½ times final salary is broadly equivalent to a scheme that provides 40/60ths.

With a money-purchase scheme, a pensioner receives a pension related to his share of the scheme at the time of retirement. The value of the fund will be affected by the amounts of employer and employee contributions and by the investment performance of the fund in the meantime. If employer and employee have each contributed 5 per cent of salary, total contributions have totalled 10 per cent a year. The pensions element of the benefits package is normally secured on retirement by the purchase of an annuity from an insurance company.

Final-salary schemes have traditionally been regarded as the Rolls-Royces of occupational schemes. From an employer's point of view, however, they represent an open-ended liability in that the employer is responsible for making up any shortfall as a result of insufficient contributions or disappointing investment outcomes. Longer life expectancy also increases the costs. Numerous employers have, as a result, closed their final-salary schemes to new members at least and provided less attractive ones based, usually, on money-purchase principles or on career average salary. Employers are transferring in this way the risk of future underfunding to their employees and there is a similar trend in the USA.

Whether or not a final-salary scheme is more beneficial than a money purchase one depends on several factors, not least the levels of contributions and the investment returns on the underlying funds. Final-salary schemes are often associated with a jobs-for-life culture that has been watered down in recent years. From the point of view of an employee, membership of a final salary scheme can inhibit job mobility because of the potential impact of changing employment on future pension benefits.

As well as pensions for members, occupational schemes may provide other benefits such as (i) pensions for widows (or widowers) and dependent children and (ii) lump sum **death-in-service** payments should an employee die before reaching normal retirement date. The precise range of benefits and their amounts vary from scheme to scheme but, prior to 6 April 2006, approved schemes could not exceed strict limits prescribed by the tax regulations.

As noted in Section 11.2, occupational schemes may or may not be contracted out of the S2P.

## 11.4 personal pensions

Personal pensions generally take the form of a contract between an employee or self-employed person and a provider such as an insurance company. They are money-purchase in that the level of benefits depends on the contributions and the investment returns in the plan. There are limits to the amounts that may be contributed although they are pretty generous. A member may not draw his benefits before age 50 (rising to 55 from 2010) whereupon he may usually take up to 25 per cent of the fund as a lump sum and the rest as pension. The pension element is typically secured through the purchase of an annuity from an insurance company.

Personal pension plans are often invested in one or more collective funds (see Section 8.5) operated by the provider. The plan-holder generally has a choice from a wide range of funds with different themes and different levels of risk.

He may also consider a **self-invested personal pension (SIPP)**, especially where substantial sums are involved (some commentators suggest £100,000 or more). A SIPP gives more flexibility over investment policy and a much wider choice of investments than a provider's collective funds. There are of course drawbacks to a DIY approach, such as lack of expertise, decisions based on emotions rather than rational thought and a failure to pursue a coherent investment strategy.

**Stakeholder pensions** are a form of personal pension plan. They have to satisfy government regulations to be stakeholder, including a condition that the annual management charges do not exceed a specified percentage of the funds under management (1½ per cent for the first ten years and 1 per cent thereafter in early 2007).

An employer of five or more people must offer access to a stakeholder pension if it does not have an occupational scheme. The employer is not required to contribute although some do, perhaps by matching employee contributions. Employees who are members of an occupational scheme may also arrange and contribute, within limits, to their own stakeholder schemes.

In addition, non-earners may contribute up to £3,600 a year (before tax relief) to a stakeholder pension. Even young children qualify for stakeholder schemes and parents or others may make contributions on their behalf with the benefit of basic-rate tax relief on the contributions. Bear in mind, however, that benefits may not be drawn until age 55 at least (or age 50 until 2010).

While the level of contributions is an obvious driver of the ultimate value of a personal plan, other critical factors include the success of the investment strategy pursued and the charges levelled against the arrangement, whether for investment functions or administration generally. An apparently small percentage of regular outgoings can have a surprisingly great effect on the performance of a plan over a period of years. Stakeholder schemes have a potential attraction in connection with charges (see above).

## 11.5 'simplification'

I have mentioned several broad categories of pension scheme but have tried to keep the description reasonably straightforward by avoiding subdivisions within those categories. I have referred also to the generous tax regimes for registered or approved schemes but again without spelling out eight separate sets of rules in place until 5 April 2006.

In an effort to simplify the tax side of things, a unified set of rules embraces all types of private (i.e. non-state) pension scheme from 6 April 2006 (known as **A day**). The distinctions between categories of pension scheme continue to apply – e.g. occupational schemes versus personal schemes – but they all fall within a single set of rules governing tax relief on contributions and the drawing of benefits. It does not mean that the subject becomes simple but it is simpler in many respects than before A day.

The new arrangements affect some people more than others. A cap on tax benefits applied from 6 April 2006 to people with a pension pot valued at £1.5 million or more. The £1.5 million translated into a pension of some £75,000 a year so the impact of the rule was likely to be relatively limited. The cap for 2007/08 is £1.6 million.

On the other hand, the vast majority of people have scope for more generous contributions than before 6 April 2006. Until then, contributions up to a proportion of earnings were permitted although the proportion varied according to circumstances.[1] Thereafter, contributions of up to 100 per cent of earnings qualify and may be made to more than one scheme. There was an initial contributions limit of £215,000 a year, a figure that was academic for most but by no means all. The limit for 2007/08 is £225,000.

The new treatment will be especially helpful to self-employed people with irregular earnings patterns and employees who have breaks in their careers (such as married women who stay at home to look after young children). In addition, non-earners may still pay up to £3,600 a year into a personal scheme and anyone earning less than £3,600 in a year has an allowance of that amount. The allowance, or balance of it, may be set against other forms of income for the purposes of income tax relief.

## 11.6  pensions reform

The government appointed a Pensions Commission chaired by Lord Adair Turner (a former leader of the Confederation of British Industries) in December 2002 to review the private pension system and long-term savings. The commission presented two reports to the government, the first in October 2004 and the second in November 2005 following an extensive consultation with government, industry and individuals on the content of the first report.

The first report described the commission's analysis of the UK pensions and retirement savings system covering the current situation, the trends in place and the challenges to be met. The second report contained the commission's specific recommendations on pensions policy.

---

1 Broadly, the limit for employee contributions to an occupational scheme was 15 per cent of earnings. For personal arrangements, the limit varied from 17.5 per cent to 40 per cent of earnings, depending on age. An earnings cap (£105,600 for 2005/06) was in place.

In the event, the commission's recommendations embraced the state schemes as well as private ones and included various options. They were controversial although it was hardly surprising in view of the scale of the crisis perceived to be looming in relation to future pensions provision and long-term savings. I reproduce in Appendix E extracts from the executive summary of the commission's first report to illustrate the 'challenges' it had identified.

The possible remedies identified by the commission included higher taxes, saving more, working longer and a combination of the three. Recommendations included changes to the state schemes to ensure an automatic subsistence income for all pensioners and the encouragement of greater savings through a **National Pensions Savings Scheme**.

The government responded through a White Paper, 'Security in Retirement: Towards a New Pensions System', published in May 2006, a Pensions Bill published in November 2006 and a further White Paper, 'Personal Accounts: A New Way to Save', published in December 2006 that built on the principles advocated by the Pensions Commission.

The Pensions Act 2007, passed in July 2007, contains the legislation to reform the state schemes:

‣ By reducing (from 6 April 2010) the number of years worked to qualify for the full basic state pension to 30 (from 44 for men and 39 for women).
‣ By introducing a system of credits to treat 'carers' as if they were working.
‣ By restoring (possibly from 2012) the index linking of the state pension to average earnings rather than retail prices inflation (earnings tend to rise faster than prices).
‣ By gradually moving the second pension from earnings-related to a flat-rate top-up to the basic pension (with implications for contracting out).
‣ By increasing the state pension age in stages to 68 by 2046.

The first four are intended to underpin the state pension as a subsistence income, notably for married women and 'carers'. The fifth has an eye on the future costs of the scheme.

To encourage saving for a pension beyond the state scheme, a further Pensions Bill was planned (at July 2007) to introduce a system of personal accounts – equivalent to the Pension Commission's National Pensions Savings Scheme – (possibly from 2012) with low running costs to which employers and the government would contribute as well as employees. Employees not in an occupational scheme would be enrolled automatically but with a right to opt out.

## 11.7 conclusions

I offer a few generalisations to try and draw the strands of the subject together.

‣ State pensions are unlikely to provide a comfortable level of income either now or in the foreseeable future. In other words, state entitlements should be supplemented by private pensions, other forms of saving or working well into one's twilight years.

- For many employees, private pension provision has traditionally taken care of itself. They have worked in occupations that have carried generous final salary schemes and employers have, in effect, assumed much of the responsibility for a comfortable income in retirement. It remains true for public sector employees but the position is changing rapidly for those in the private sector. Final salary schemes are becoming an endangered species outside the public sector.

- For the self-employed, the onus has always been on the individual, although he now has greater flexibility over contributions and the methods of investing his scheme. Similar considerations apply to those who conduct their business through family companies.

- Money-purchase occupational schemes and personal pension plans place the risk of poor investment performance on the members rather than on the employer. Hence, holders of personal plans especially need to consider carefully both their levels of contribution and the choice of investments. Consistently good investment returns can make a vast difference to financial wellbeing in retirement.

- The primary purpose of pensions provision is to provide an income in retirement. It is not the only way, however, and accumulating wealth in other ways should also be considered. For instance, pensions schemes attract reliefs in relation to both contributions and their investment returns but are relatively inflexible over the drawing of benefits. ISAs do not attract tax relief on contributions but are extremely versatile in other ways. Many people see the acquisition of buy-to-let properties as a retirement nest egg. Some sort of balance is desirable.

- Employees should consider what is on offer from their employers. An employer will contribute to an occupational scheme and its running costs while an employee can consider topping up its benefits either by AVCs or by setting up a supplementary scheme of his own. Even where there is no occupational scheme, an employer who offers access to a stakeholder plan may also agree to contribute. In addition, the administration costs may be lower for the employee than if he arranges a plan himself.

- A self-employed person can, in effect, smooth out fluctuations in his profits by increasing contributions to a personal scheme in years of plenty and reducing them in years of famine. If he employs an accountant, it is desirable if not essential to involve the accountant in decisions over contribution levels.

- Anyone who is relying on a personal plan should watch the costs like a hawk. The costs may appear to be a small percentage but they can prove a considerable drag on the investment returns over the long term. Where collective funds are involved, the management charges of stakeholder schemes are capped and the charges for tracker funds are generally lower than for actively managed funds (see also Section 8.5). In addition, the running costs of some of the generalist investment trusts are relatively low and the trusts are worth considering as long-term core investments.

▸ An option with personal plans, particularly for larger amounts, is SIPPs. People looking for an active involvement in the investment side or a flexible approach generally should consider self-administration of this nature. Pay attention, nonetheless, to the costs of establishing and running the SIPP and to investment charges especially if collective investments are involved. There can also be practical drawbacks with a DIY approach.

*buying a home*

introduction – methods of ownership – finance for house purchase – 'homework' – household insurance – taxation – the processes on a typical purchase

## 12.1 introduction

Buying a home embraces aspects of personal finance as well as other disciplines including land law. I remind you also of my remarks in Section 4.6 on land and buildings as a form of wealth. I am concerned here with ownership of homes for personal occupation rather than as investments to generate an income or for capital profit. Nonetheless, home ownership has been highly profitable over the years even though its primary purpose has been to put a roof over the head.

The proportion of people in Britain owning their own homes has risen relentlessly since the end of the Second World War. Before then, ordinary mortals often had to rent as they did not have the finance to buy. The availability of affordable, long-term loans from building societies and banks has contributed greatly to the boom in home-ownership.

The main purpose of this section is to outline the considerations, particularly the financial ones, in acquiring and, to a point, owning your own home. The purchase of a house is the largest transaction that many people undertake during their lives although the capitalised value of their pension benefits may in fact be considerably more.

## 12.2 methods of ownership

I drew a distinction in Section 4.6 between freehold and leasehold estates in land (including the buildings erected on them). I think it fair to say that most twenty-first-century householders own the freehold. Important exceptions relate to flats and apartments, many of which continue to be held on long leaseholds for legal reasons.

Another distinction is between sole and joint ownership. At one time, husbands tended to buy the family home in their sole names and their wives were particularly vulnerable if marital relationships deteriorated or husbands failed to make adequate provision by will for their widows.

Nowadays, joint ownership by spouses, partners and others who choose to pool their resources is largely the norm. Whatever the relationship, it is highly desirable that the documents of title spell out the extent of the beneficial interests of the respective parties.

In addition, the nature of the beneficial interests determines what happens to the share of a co-owner on his (her) death. Thus, if H and W own Rose Cottage as beneficial joint tenants, the entire beneficial interest accrues to the survivor on the first death; if H dies first, W becomes the sole owner regardless of the terms of H's will and vice versa. If, on the other hand, they own Rose Cottage as tenants in common (whether in equal shares or otherwise) and H dies first, H's share passes under the terms of his will; W may or may not be the beneficiary.

Remember too that the contents of a house and other chattels (see Section 2.13) are separate from the land and buildings (unless they amount to fixtures or fittings). The ownership of the two classes of assets need not coincide although they often do in practice.

## 12.3 finance for house purchase

Clearly, the purchaser of a house can finance the transaction in a number of ways and he will often combine two or more methods. He may have savings on a bank deposit or other saleable assets such as company shares or another house. If he needs to borrow, he may do so from private individuals (parents for instance) or from a commercial lender such as a bank or building society.

Chapter 5 is devoted to borrowing generally. With buying a house, the facility is typically long term (20–25 years) and the loan secured by a mortgage over the property acquired. Other considerations include the amount the lender is prepared to advance against the value of the property, the rate of interest and the programme for repayment.

I alluded in Section 5.3 to the distinction between repayment loans and interest-only loans. With the former, the monthly payments comprise elements of interest and capital so that the outstanding balance of the mortgage reduces steadily. With the latter, the homeowner pays interest only to the lender but looks to another asset, often an endowment policy, to repay the loan in due course.

With-profits endowment policies (discussed also in Section 6.4) are a form of investment and, in recent years, their returns have often fallen short of those projected when the policy was being negotiated. As a result, there have been insufficient funds to meet complete repayment of the loan when it has fallen due. The so-called endowment mortgage mis-selling scandal featured prominently in the newspaper headlines for several years.

The moral of the story relates essentially to risk. With a repayment mortgage, the loan runs off automatically provided that the borrower keeps up his monthly payments thoroughout the term of the mortgage. With an interest-only mortgage, there is the danger that the endowment policy (or other investment) will not meet expectations leaving part of the loan uncovered on maturity and a need to find a shortfall from other resources.

Equivalent considerations apply to more exotic forms of loan notably **flexible**, **offset** and **current-account** mortgages. It may be convenient to defer payments for a period but, sooner or later, the lender will require reductions in the loan.

An even more sophisticated variation is mortgages linked to pension-fund entitlements for repayment. In the absence of very special circumstances, I consider it highly desirable to keep the purchase of a house and the accumulation of a future source of income entirely separate.

Another avenue of finance is a **shared-equity scheme** – a form of co-ownership – either with a private individual (parent, etc) or a commercial partner. It means of course that, when the house is sold, the other party is entitled to a proportion of the proceeds leaving less for the purchase of another property or whatever. You should consider all the implications and take good advice before entering into such a transaction. Where relatives are involved, there can be awkward tax considerations and, with commercial arrangements, you are concerned with the potential costs among the issues to be ironed out.

I look later at legal steps such as contract and completion. Suffice it say at this point that you need to have your finance lined up, including a specific commitment from a commercial lender, before entering into a binding contract to buy.

## 12.4 'homework'

My perspective here is buying a house, particularly for the first time. There are parallel processes with selling and, if you move house, you will probably be faced with both selling and buying.

I divide the homework into three lines of enquiry: practical aspects, purchase costs, running costs. I recommend working through them conscientiously and, in any event, before entering into a legally binding deal.

### practical aspects

The focus is on the house that you propose to buy. In undertaking your research, it is worth adopting the principle of *caveat emptor* or let the buyer beware, whether or not it is strictly necessary. In other words, be proactive in your investigations and, where possible, check out the assertions of the seller and anyone acting for him (including an estate agent).

Most house-buyers need to employ agents of their own for certain tasks, notably a solicitor or other qualified person for the **conveyancing** (legal work) and a surveyor to report, among other things, on the condition of the property and matters affecting it. Even so, there is scope to undertake reasonably extensive homework of your own before incurring professional charges. A thorough physical inspection should give you a fair idea of the state of repair while enquiries of the local authority may alert you to plans for a new road at the bottom of the garden.

Broadly, you are concerned to ensure that the property is suitable for your needs in terms of location, accommodation, amenities, age, character and state of repair. Location is intended to take in the nature of the neighbourhood, the access to schools and other local services as well as the proximity to public transport.

## purchase costs

At the time of writing (early 2007), the average value of a house in England is around £200,000. The total costs involved in acquiring and moving to such a house are, however, significantly more. Relatively few first-time buyers can afford a house of £200,000 but the figure is a nice round one to work with.

SDLT of 1 per cent payable by a purchaser amounts to £2,000 and legal and survey fees are likely to account for another £1,000–£2,000. Further direct costs include Land Registry charges, search fees and a commercial lender's arrangement fee. Estate agents generally act for sellers so their commission should not be an issue.

Where charges are at stake, obtain competitive quotations and agree them in writing before engaging the agent. A solicitor's charge, for instance, should depend on the amount of work involved, so it may be necessary to agree a qualified figure at the outset.

Be careful over the scope of a survey. A typical bank or building society report and valuation is prepared for the lender and is not a thorough survey of the condition of the property for a prospective owner. Depending on the age and state of the property, a would-be buyer should obtain a more extensive survey and, to avoid duplication, seek to arrange with the lender a single document that covers both purposes.

Indirect costs relate to removal and other incidental charges as well as the costs of equipping the new home with carpets, curtains, furniture and other home comforts. Some items may of course be bought from the seller.

The direct and indirect costs over and above the basic purchase price could easily amount to 10 per cent (i.e. £20,000 for £200,000) or more. In terms of the mortgage limit, a lender's criteria will include the value of the house but the lender may add its own arrangement fee to the loan. Consumer credit is often available for consumer goods but will come at a price!

I should mention for completeness **Home Information Packs** or **(HIPs)**. The following was taken from a government website:[1]

> From 1 June 2007, all home owners in England and Wales will need to prepare a Home Information Pack before putting their home up for sale.
>
> The Home Information Pack is a set of documents providing important

---

1 www.direct.gov.uk/HomeAndCommunity/BuyingAndSellingYourHome/ServicesForPropertyBuyers
AndSellers/PropertyServicesArticles/fs/en?Content_ID=10026751&chk=0s3xsu

information about a property such as searches, copies of the deeds and a new document called the Home Condition Report, which assesses the condition of a property and its energy efficiency.

Currently, much of this essential information only comes to light when an offer has been made and accepted. In the meantime, buyers are negotiating in the dark and are often wasting money on legal fees, searches and surveys.

Providing all the information up front, at the time of marketing a property, will make the home buying and selling process more efficient and transparent.

The proposals were contentious from the outset. In essence, they switched some of the onus on a buyer to discover information to a seller to volunteer it but at a cost of several hundreds of pounds to the seller. The most costly element was the Home Condition Report (a survey) and the government amended (seriously watered down!) the proposals in July 2006 by making its inclusion in the pack voluntary.[1]

## running costs

Once you are installed, there is the little matter of keeping the place up and running. It is as well to check that you will be able to do so as part of your homework.

The direct costs of running the house include:

- mortgage payments (interest and, where appropriate, capital);
- premiums on an endowment policy if you have adopted that method of repayment;
- the insurance premiums for buildings and contents cover;
- heating, lighting, water, council tax;
- rent (if leasehold);
- repairs and maintenance.

It is usually possible to make reasonable estimates of each item if precise figures are not available and desirable to overestimate rather than underestimate. In the case of mortgage interest, you should factor in any possibility that the rate of interest may increase.

Improvements such as building an extension are further capital expenditure rather than running costs. Hence they are probably best evaluated as separate projects.

Indirect costs include items such as premiums for life assurance, family income benefit, mortgage payment protection and critical illness. They do not relate to the property itself but provide a fallback for the mortgage and other outgoings should things go badly wrong. Chapter 6 is devoted generally to

---

1 On 22 May 2007, the government made a further U-turn. It deferred the start date of HIPS to 1 August 2007 and confined their operation for the time being to homes with four or more bedrooms.

insurance and assurance and I direct the next section specifically to home and contents insurance.

## 12.5 household insurance

Ideally, the structure should be insured against a wide range of contingencies – fire, storm, lightning, flood, explosion, earthquake, impact, water damage, vandalism, theft, subsidence, heave, third-party claims, etc. There are numerous policies on offer and I prefer value for money from a reputable provider rather than the cheapest option from an obscure entity. Some mortgage companies seek to tie you to their own insurances but I would be wary of such tactics. Whoever the insurer is, obtain a copy of the policy document and read it carefully before committing yourself.

The insurance value of the buildings is not necessarily the market value of the entire premises; among other things, the premises include the land. You are looking mainly at rebuilding costs (usually quoted at so many pounds per square foot or square metre) plus site clearance and architect's fees on the assumption of a total loss.

Similarly, with contents you should be considering a wide range of risks and, ideally, a policy that covers items for their replacement value (new for old) rather than for their depreciated value (i.e. their value at the time of the claim). A comprehensive list of your possessions and some basic arithmetic should suffice to work out a suitable total – and it soon mounts up. Most insurers offer cover for buildings and contents on the same policy with the advantage that you need deal with only one insurer. If, however, you have unusual contents, perhaps an important collection of antique scrubbing brushes, you may need to obtain a professional valuation and consider a specialist insurer. You may also be entering the realms of inventories, photographs and burglar alarms.

Insurance policies generally contain a warranty against under-insurance with correspondingly low premiums from the insurer's point of view. Under insurance can be a false economy as, in the event of a claim, the insurer will be looking to abate the amount it will pay out whether or not there has been a total loss. On occasion, the insurer may resist a claim completely.

Policies often contain an escalator clause under which the cover increases automatically in line with specified price indices. Even so, you should satisfy yourself that your cover is adequate at least annually or in the event of a material change in circumstances, e.g. an improvement to the property or the acquisition of some valuable contents. In addition, an insurance policy is a contract made in 'utmost good faith' so that you should inform your insurer promptly of anything that may have a bearing on the risks insured against.

## 12.6 taxation

Chapter 7 is directed at various forms of taxation and I attempt here to put them in the context of a homeowner.

*Income Tax*: homeowners do not pay tax on a notional value of their occupation but, equally, they do not generally qualify for tax relief on mortgage interest paid. If they cease to occupy the property and rent it out, they are liable to income tax on the profits of the letting.

*Capital Gains Tax*: as noted in Section 7.3, there is an exemption for the disposal (sale, etc.) of a person's principal private residence. The exemption is reduced where the owner has not been in residence throughout the period of ownership. Only one exemption is available to spouses and civil partners. Where there is ownership of two or more houses, the taxpayer should nominate one as his principal residence.

*Inheritance Tax*: a house, whether occupied or let, is an asset in a person's estate for IHT purposes. Hence, the value is brought into account on his death (unless an exemption, such as for benefits to a spouse, applies). The considerable rise in the value of houses in recent years has rendered more estates liable to the tax.

Not surprisingly, some intrepid taxpayers have engaged in highly ingenious schemes to avoid or reduce IHT attributable to their houses. HMRC has strenuously challenged many of the ploys and promoted changes in the legislation. Effective IHT planning with one's house is a tortuous area and should only be attempted with the best of professional advice.

*Stamp Duty Land Tax*: refer to Section 7.7.

*Council Tax*: refer to Section 7.8.

## 12.7 the processes on a typical purchase

All transactions are individual but most buyers need to follow a typical sequence of steps. I round off this section with an outline of the process that one might expect. The points are not necessarily in chronological order and several things may be happening at the same time.

- Track down a suitable property – it involves a trawl of local newspapers, estate agents, websites and personal recommendations. Do not forget that estate agents are generally acting for the vendors.
- Do your homework (see Section 12.4).
- Negotiate a price and any other important terms – usually through the vendor's estate agent. Take care to conduct all negotiations subject to contract and subject to survey to avoid becoming legally committed prematurely.
- Arrange mortgage finance – shop around or go to a mortgage broker. You will need a specific commitment before you enter into a binding contract to buy. Make sure you have funds available to pay the deposit on exchange of contracts (see below).

- Engage a solicitor – if need be shop around and agree a fee. Issue formal instructions once you have agreed terms with the buyer or his agent.
- Arrange for a survey – consider carefully the depth of survey that you require; if need be, shop around for a suitable surveyor and agree a fee. Ideally, one survey should cover both your requirements and those of the lender.
- Correspond with your solicitor over the pre-contract enquiries and any special terms of the transaction (e.g. the purchase of contents from the vendor). Other matters are the dates for the exchange of contracts and for completion.
- Arrange insurance cover for the buildings and contents (see Section 12.5). The buildings cover needs to start on exchange of contracts while the contents cover should start when you enter into occupation (on or after completion).
- Exchange of contracts – you become bound on the purchase at this point and, if you pull out without completing, you are likely to lose your deposit and possibly be liable to the vendor for further sums. Traditionally, a 10 per cent deposit is payable on exchange of contracts but the matter is one for negotiation between the parties.
- Completion – this usually takes place a few weeks after the exchange of contracts on a date stipulated in the contract. The balance of the purchase price is due and the vendor's solicitor will arrange for the keys to be handed over once he has the funds. The buyer is then free to take possession.
- Title deeds – the mortgage company will hold the originals but the buyer may have copies. He should also retain his insurance policy and other important documents in a safe and convenient place.

## growing old gracefully

introduction – health and care issues – wealth issues – taxation issues – capacity issues – conflicts of interest

## 13.1 introduction

The focus of this chapter is on the elderly and, to a point, infirm. Figures published by the Office of National Statistics following the 2001 census show that the UK population has aged considerably since the 1951 census:

| Approximate trend | 1951 | 2001 |
|---|---|---|
| Total population – up by a sixth | 50.2m | 58.8m |
| Proportion aged under 16 – down by a sixth | 24% | 20% |
| Proportion aged 60 and over – up by a third | 16% | 21% |
| Proportion aged 85 and over – up five times | 0.4% | 1.9% |

The ageing reflects longer life expectancy as a result of improvements in living standards and health care. The trend is expected to continue; even by 2001, there were more people of 60 and over than there were children under 16.

Although I am writing about old age, my perspective is also from the point of view of younger people who have responsibilities in relation to parents and possibly other ageing relatives. The tasks of supporting such people can be extremely stressful both emotionally and practically. I cannot offer much in terms of emotional support but I hope the following remarks will help in relation to the practical challenges of personal finance.

Once again, the scope of the subject is enormous and I confine myself to setting the scene. A number of the sections are really extensions of earlier chapters in the book and deal with specific issues likely to arise with people in or approaching their twilight years. In addition, some of the issues can prove complex and require specific advice from specialist professionals.

An advantage of growing old for some – but not all – is the prospect of retirement from working life, giving more time for relaxation and greater opportunities for travel and other pursuits that have in the past taken second place. It helps considerably to have a sufficient level of income to maintain comfortably such a lifestyle, and capital to call on should the need arise.

At the same time, many will encounter sooner or later one or more challenges of old age.[1] I divide them into four limbs: wealth, health, personal care and residential care.

*Wealth* is about the material resources of income and capital. In terms of income, it helps to have a good occupational or personal pension as the state schemes provide for subsistence at best. Pensions, however, are income by nature and devoid of accessible capital. At the other extreme, many people of retirement age have valuable houses free of a mortgage but such assets rarely provide an income or ready access to capital.

An advantage of owning income-yielding assets – bank deposits, stocks, shares, rented properties, etc – is that they both generate an income and constitute a store of capital. There is also the flexibility to switch from one asset type to another as circumstances change.

*Health* is about the condition of the body and the mind. Like machines, they need to be kept in good working order and body parts have a habit of wearing out.

*Personal care* is about the routine tasks of keeping alive – getting out of bed, washing, dressing, preparing food, eating, drinking, shopping, cleaning, entertaining yourself, getting into bed. It is easy to take such things for granted until they become difficult or impossible.

*Residential care* is about where and how you live and is a stage on from personal care. Can you continue in your present home, with or without help? Can you move to another home of your own that is more suitable for your needs? Have you reached a point where it is impossible for you to continue to live in a home of your own?

These themes are the foundations for the remaining sections of this chapter. Wealth issues are an important determinant of what is possible and what is not. I start, therefore, with health and care issues in Section 13.2 and devote the following sections to wealth and related topics.

## 13.2 health and care issues

It may help to consider a few scenarios that involve an older person:

▸ He (or she) lives in his own home but needs medical treatment either as an out-patient or an in-patient. He may be an out-patient of a primary care provider (such as a general practitioner or a dentist) or of a secondary care

---

1 A report Dementia UK prepared for the Alzheimer's Society and published in early 2007 contained some revealing data on the prevalence of dementia in elderly people. See www.alzheimers.org.uk.

provider (such as a hospital). He would normally be an in-patient of a hospital because of the need to stay in for an operation or other complex procedure.

- He lives in his own home but needs help with personal care and, perhaps, health care.
- He is unable to continue in his own home so moves to a residential home for accommodation and personal care.
- He is unable to continue in his own home and has a medical condition that necessitates accommodation in a care home coupled with nursing attention.

A member of the public is naturally concerned to know what he has to pay for and what is provided by the state. From a political point of view, it is helpful to make a distinction between (i) medical treatment and nursing care and (ii) personal care and residential care.

Medical and nursing matters generally fall within the ambit of the National Health Service (NHS) whereas personal care and residential care are matters primarily for local authorities. The fact that separate government agencies – the NHS and local authorities – may be involved, coupled with different rules on funding, adds to life's complications.

## medical treatment and nursing care

Much of the treatment provided by the NHS is free in the sense that users do not have to make a direct payment. There are of course costs, the bulk of which we meet indirectly through the taxation system. There are also exceptions to the principle of free treatment, for example with dental charges and prescription charges (albeit that various groups of people are exempted from paying them).

The scope of NHS treatment is, in theory at least, pretty comprehensive. Even so, high-profile cases over whether or not an NHS trust should meet the costs of certain treatments make the headlines from time to time. NHS waiting times have impeded access to in-patient treatment in particular and the government has spent a lot of money to reduce them.

In the meantime, there has been growth in private health care provision financed to a significant extent by private medical insurance. Many employers arrange cover for their employees through group schemes and former employees often have an opportunity to continue cover on relatively attractive terms when they retire.

As to residents of care homes that provide nursing care, the NHS is responsible for meeting the cost of the care provided by registered nurses through **continuing care** and **registered nursing care contribution** (RNCC). A person assessed as qualifying for continuing care receives the entire cost of the care and no means test is involved. Eligibility for fully funded health care is governed by local criteria and there have been cases of controversy over the narrowness of criteria set by some authorities (to which I return under 'Issues' below). With RNCC, a person is assessed at one of three levels of need and receives a contribution to his fees accordingly (see also Section 13.3 under Health care benefits).

## personal care and residential care

An even greater concern tends to be with the costs of personal care and residential care. The scenarios above illustrate that personal care may be an issue whether or not a person lives in his own home while further issues over residential care arise when a person cannot continue in his own home.

Conventional wisdom encourages people to retain independence in their own homes for as long as practicable. Arguably, it gives them more reason to be and it is less costly than residential care. In some cases, relatives or even friends act as carers to help with day-to-day functions. In others, the person relies on the services of paid carers arranged either through the local authority or independently. Wardened accommodation is another possibility, notably for people reliant on paid support.

People who need such personal care should consider claiming **attendance allowance** (see Section 13.3 'Welfare benefits'). In addition, **carer's allowance** is a benefit for people who meet a number of criteria including the provision of 35 hours a week of care.

Residential care can be arranged either through the local authority or privately. A local authority will assess whether or not a person needs a place based on criteria it has set. When it comes to costs, however, they are means-tested and residents with capital over £21,500 (from 9 April 2007) are expected to meet the full costs of personal care and residential care. For people with capital below £13,000, there is a contribution from income but not capital. Between £13,000 and £21,500, contributions from income and capital are expected.[1]

A house is generally regarded as a capital asset for this purpose and it may therefore have to be sold to cover the cost of care. It is disregarded, however, if occupied by a partner or certain other relatives. In addition, anti-avoidance rules allow local authorities to bring into account assets given away to circumvent the means-testing.

## issues

The obligations over health care and social care (embracing personal care and residential care) are not always clear-cut in practice as was illustrated by two important court cases, Coughlan in 1999 and Grogan in 2006. The issue in both concerned the extent of the responsibilities of the NHS given that health care was free and social care was means-tested.

Age Concern, the Alzheimer's Society, Help the Aged and the Royal College of Nursing produced a leaflet 'Guide to Fully Funded NHS Care' in March 2006 available on www.ageconcern.org.uk in conjunction with Nicola Mackintosh of Mackintosh Duncan solicitors who acted for Mrs Coughlan in the earlier case.

---

1 The local authority charging procedures are governed by the 'Charging for Residential Accommodation' (CRAG) published on the Department of Health website www.dh.gov.uk under 'Policy and Guidance'.

The aim of the bodies concerned was 'to help people in need of services, their carers, and professionals working in health and social care to know when the NHS is responsible for paying the full cost of packages of care'.

The guide explains that the NHS is legally responsible for providing, on occasion, a care package that includes an element of social care as well as health care and to meet the entire cost without means-testing or charging. In addition, the NHS should meet the cost of health care that includes an element of social care for someone in their own home where their condition (physical or mental) warrants it.

The High Court judge in the Grogan case (2006) criticised the Department of Health for failing to produce clear guidance to the NHS. The situation was further complicated by the degree of delegation to local Primary Care Trusts.

There had been a similar criticism by the Health Service Ombudsman in her report 'NHS Funding for Long-term Care' (HC399) published in February 2003. The Parliamentary and Health Service Ombudsman report 'Retrospective Continuing Care Funding and Redress' (HC 386) dated 13 March 2007 contained further findings of maladministration by the Department of Health and by NHS Primary Care Trusts. The Department of Health had issued formal guidance from time to time to Strategic Health Authorities, Primary Care Trusts and local authorities and its further guidance to Primary Care Trusts 'NHS Continuing Care Redress' of 14 March 2007 was in response to the Ombudsman's report dated the previous day.[1] Is it fair to conclude that there is a tension between, on the one hand, the political expedient of being seen to provide 'free' health care and, on the other, an unwillingness or inability to pay for it?

Turning to social care, the Commission for Social Care Inspectorate published its annual report The State of Social Care in England 2005/06 in January 2007, available at www.csci.org.uk. The report covered all social care and found that local authorities were tightening their rules about who qualified for state-funded care. As for older and disabled people, more were having to arrange and fund private care themselves or rely on family and friends. I quote too some telling statistics from the press release: 'Recent projections indicate a rise of 53% in the number of older people with some care needs over the next twenty years; and a rise of 54% in older people with a high level of need.'

## arranging care

When faced with arranging care for an elderly person, I suggest the following lines of enquiry. If a medical condition is involved, you should consult initially with the patient's general practitioner over a medical assessment for continuing care or RNCC. Individual cases turn on their merits so that professional help may be desirable at some stage. Subject to that, you should approach the local authority for an assessment of personal care and residential care needs.

---

1 See www.dh.gov.uk – Policy and Guidance – Organisation Policy – Integrated Care – Continuing Care and www.ombudsman.org.uk/improving_services/special_reports/index.html).

There may be the option of – if not the necessity for – independent provision, but explore the state channels first. An advantage of staying within the system is that there are fewer complications if there is a need to apply for local authority assistance later or if there is a move from one local authority area to another.

Comprehensive information is available from local authorities and the charities interested in this field. I include some further details in Further reading and resources.

## 13.3 wealth issues

### own wealth

Chapters 8 and 9 looked at investing money and my concern here is with its application to older people. I assume for this purpose a significant level of **free assets**, i.e. material wealth beyond a principal residence, its contents, a car and other belongings necessary for day-to-day living.

Section 8.8 on investment policy includes remarks on liquid reserves, capital growth versus income yield and building a portfolio which are directed to acquiring a range of investments suitable to one's circumstances. How might these criteria apply in the context of this chapter?

**Liquid reserves** are money readily available for unforeseen expenditures. In addition, it is desirable to set aside reserves for planned future expenditure such as an expensive holiday, medical treatment to be funded privately, a gift to a child, the purchase of a new car, a house move.

**Capital growth versus income yield** is a starting point for formulating investment policy once sufficient has been earmarked as reserves. A driving issue is how much immediate income is needed from the investment portfolio to supplement any pensions, casual earnings, etc. Arriving at a figure is likely to involve some sort of budgeting exercise.

At the same time, a view is needed on what income is likely to be required in the future. Experience suggests that inflation will continue so that, regardless of individual circumstances, an increasing level of income is desirable and should be factored in.

**Building a portfolio** comes down to specific choices of investments including whether or not existing holdings continue to meet one's needs. Past policy might have been to seek capital growth on the footing that earnings provided sufficient to live on, any income from savings would be taxed heavily and the emphasis should be on building up capital for the future.

If income has dropped as a result of leaving work, investment income may be of greater importance and, in any case, time profiles are likely to be shorter. Policy bias may change from capital growth to high immediate income or an intermediate steadily increasing income with some potential for capital growth.

Issues such as care in one's own home or in a residential home are likely to have a significant bearing on investment strategy and are best planned for if possible. In some instances, the sale of the person's home may provide an additional source of funding and another avenue for investigation is long-term care insurance, referred to below.

income from the state

## state pension

I outlined the state pension scheme in Section 11.2. Men become entitled to their state pension from age 65 and, for women, a change from 60 to 65 is being phased in. The basic pension is generally related to one's NICs record whereas the S2P is based on earnings-related contributions for employees not contracted out.

The maximum basic state pension per week for the 52 weeks from 09 April 2007 is:

| | |
|---|---|
| Based on own or late partner's NICs | £87.30 |
| Based on partner's NICs | £52.30 |
| Addition for over 80s | £0.25 |
| Over-80s non-contributory pension | £52.30 |

The state pension is administered by the Pension Service of the Department of Work and Pensions (DWP).

## pension credits

Pension credits are available to underpin the income of people of 60 or over on low incomes. For the year 2007/08, pension credit (**guarantee credit**) is likely to be available if weekly income is less than:

| | |
|---|---|
| single person | £119.05 |
| partners | £181.70 |

For people of 65 and over with modest savings, investments or income, pension credit (**savings credit**) may be available where weekly income is up to (for 2007/08):

| | |
|---|---|
| single person | £166.60 |
| partners | £244.85 |

The weekly limits of savings credit are £19.05 for a single person and £25.26 for partners.

The Pension Service of the DWP administers pension credits.

The credit for people of 60 and over arguably reduces the incentive to save to generate an income up to the guaranteed figure. If the state is going to provide for you, why make the effort yourself?[1]

---

1 Against this, government reforms are designed to bolster the state scheme as a subsistence income and introduce greater incentives for saving for pensions on top of the state scheme (see Section 11.6). They may result in less reliance on supplementary benefits and individuals should draw their own conclusions.

## welfare benefits

Apart from the state pension, **welfare benefits** such as attendance allowance, disability living allowance, housing benefit and council tax benefit may be applicable and are not taken into account for the purposes of pension credit.

Attendance allowance applies to people over 65 who need help with bodily functions and it is not means-tested. There are two rates, £64.50 a week for day and night help and £43.15 a week for day or night only help. The rates quoted are for 2007/08. Disability living allowance is similar except that it applies to people under 65 who need care. The Disability and Carers Service of the DWP handles the allowances.

Housing and council tax benefits fall within the province of local authorities.

## health care benefits

I referred in Section 13.2 to NHS continuing care and RNCC. From 9 April 2007, the RNCC levels in England are:

| Band | Amount (per week) |
|---|---|
| High – frequent nurse input | £139 |
| Medium – daily nurse input | £87 |
| Low – minimal nurse input | £40 |

## private funding schemes

I outline three of relevance to this chapter.

### private medical insurance (PMI)

PMI is a means to help bypass NHS waiting lists through the funding of private treatment. Such treatment may also provide a wider choice of consultant and more salubrious conditions than with the NHS. Hence, PMI is something of an expensive luxury with a tendency for annual premiums to rise more quickly than the rate of retail price inflation. It is difficult to quote figures for premium levels because they vary with circumstances and the level of cover chosen.

Policy cover ranges from **comprehensive** for the full works to **low-cost options** with more limited benefits. The budget variants may, for instance, limit the level of hospital accommodation and require the policy-holder to use NHS treatment if it can be arranged within a specified time such as six weeks. Most aim to provide cover for the diagnosis and treatment of non-emergency, acute conditions.

Premiums reflect age, locality and past medical history. Policies may be written on a family basis but they often exclude existing medical conditions for which a policy member has had treatment within a specified period of years.

Other features may include no-claims discounts and high excesses that the policy-holder meets himself. One strategy is to self-fund less expensive private treatments but to look to insure for dearer treatments.

### long-term care insurance

This type of insurance recognises that personal care and residential care benefits are means-tested and that the annual fees of a private care home can easily amount to £25,000 (I base the figure on a report in the FT of 15–16 April 2006 on long-term care). Long-term care insurance is a relatively recent innovation and is available through a few specialist providers.

Policies fall into two main categories:

1 the cover is pre-funded through regular contributions;
2 the cover is paid for by a lump sum investment when a person moves to a care home.

With the former, the policyholder can claim when he is no longer able to carry out 'activities of daily living' such as washing, dressing, feeding, mobility and continence. The cover may be designed for care in one's own home or in a residential home.

The latter takes the form of an annuity based on the policyholder's age, sex, health and other factors. As with annuities generally, it protects against longevity but can prove a frustrating investment if the annuitant fails to meet his expectation of life.

### home income plans

I referred in Section 5.3 to equity release and the availability of schemes for elderly people who own their own homes but are short of income. Such schemes are available through a few specialist providers and I recommend the taking of independent advice before committing oneself to such a scheme.

The following two sections deal with derivatives of wealth issues.

## 13.4 taxation issues

The remarks in this section extend the content of Chapter 7.

### income tax

I referred in Section 7.2 to the personal allowance and specified the rate for persons under 65. There are higher personal allowances for people of 65 to 74 and of 75 and over and the rates for 2007/08 are:

| Personal allowance 2007/08 | Amount |
|---|---|
| Standard level (to age 64) | £5,225 |
| Age 65 to 74 | £7,550 |
| Age 75 or over | £7,690 |

The higher allowance is reduced, however, if income exceeds £20,900. It drops £1 for every £2 excess income to bring it back to the standard level. As a result, persons of 65-74 pay a marginal rate of tax of 33 per cent on income between £20,900 and £25,550 and persons of 75 and over pay 33 per cent on income between £20,900 and £25,830.

The married couples' allowance was abolished generally in 2000 but a form of it is still available to married couples where either spouse was born before 6 April 1935. The allowance for 2007/08 is £6,285 for ages 65 to 74 and £6,365 for ages 75 and over. It is limited to 10 per cent and is partly clawed back where an individual's income exceeds £20,900. A husband may elect to transfer the allowance to his wife if his income is insufficient to use it himself. The allowance is adapted for marriages on or after 5 December 2005 and civil partnerships by allocating the allowance to the partner with the higher income unless there is an election otherwise.

### Capital Gains Tax

It may be helpful to look back to Section 7.3 for an introduction to CGT.

There are important reliefs for owners of **business property** who make gifts or sales. Business property is defined to include assets used in a trade, unquoted shares in a trading company and certain holdings of agricultural land.

In the event of a gift to which the relief applies, the deemed disposal takes place on a 'no gain, no loss' basis with the donee being treated as inheriting at the donor's acquisition value. The idea is that, if the donee subsequently sells, the gain relieved on the gift is brought back into a charge to tax.

If the owner sells a business asset that has been held for at least two years, **taper relief** can bring the effective rate of tax on a gain down to 10 per cent. I should stress that these explanations are oversimplifications and that careful consideration of the tax is needed in practice.

### Inheritance Tax

Section 7.5 contained an outline that I supplement with the following points on gifts, reliefs and planning that may be of particular interest to older people and their families. The exemptions are available to both partners.

- Normal expenditure out of income – regular gifts out of the donor's income are exempt provided that he is left with sufficient income for his normal standard of living (taking one year with another).
- Small gifts – gifts totalling up to £250 per individual in a tax year are exempt; qualifying gifts may be made to any number of individuals.
- Annual exemption – applies to the first £3,000 of gifts (not otherwise exempted) in a tax year; it may be applied to a larger gift; if unused in year one, it may be carried forward to year two only and used after the exemption for year two.
- Gifts to registered charities – they are exempt.
- Potentially exempt transfers – certain non-exempt, irrevocable gifts are not taxed on the making of the gift but, if the donor dies within seven

years, they are then brought into account and taxed as the 'first slice' of the donor's estate.

- Reservation of benefit – a gift is ineffective for tax purposes if the donor does not relinquish full enjoyment; for example, a father gives his house to his son and then continues to live there rent-free.
- **Agricultural property relief, business property relief** – the underlying principle is to reduce (in some cases to nil) the value of qualifying property for the purposes of the tax. The definition of business property is directed to trading assets as opposed to purely investment ones. Strict conditions apply and professional advice is desirable.
- Houses – the scope for planning to reduce IHT on private residences is now extremely limited. For those determined to do so, professional advice is a must and is likely to be expensive. Consider 'trading down' and giving away some of the proceeds.
- **Generation-skipping** – for grandparents with wealthy children, consider making gifts direct to, or for the benefit of, grandchildren thus bypassing the estates of the children.
- Careful drafting of wills generally – wills often provide scope for IHT avoidance. Spouses and other partners should consider their wills in tandem. See also the example in Section 7.5.
- Health warning – if making gifts to avoid tax, the donor should leave himself and his partner with sufficient resources to live out the rest of their days comfortably.

## 13.5  capacity issues

**Capacity** in this context is about legal competence rather than the size of a container. It crops up routinely in connection with wills but it is of far wider import. Generally, a person is legally competent to enter into a transaction only if he has the capacity or state of mind to do so.

Mental capacity is easier to recognise than to define in many respects. Loss of capacity may be sudden, perhaps as a result of an accident, or may be gradual such as with the onset of dementia in older people. Often people are able to do simple day-to-day tasks but not more complex ones like handling financial matters. If things get bad enough, one should seek the advice of a doctor or other health professional for an opinion or formal assessment.

### wills and trusts

An important case is that of Banks v Goodfellow of 1870 (L.R. 5 QB 549) and is one that has been quoted in more recent cases such as Sharp & Bryson v Adam & Adam of 2006 (EWCA Civ 449). The Banks case contains the 'golden rule' of testamentary capacity.

The court held that, for a person to have testamentary capacity, he had to satisfy four tests. I paraphrase the first three as:

1  an understanding of the nature of a will and the effect of making one;
2  an understanding of the extent and nature of the property covered by the will;
3  an understanding of the people whom he should consider benefitting and their respective claims on his estate.

I cannot resist quoting an extract from the judgement with the fourth test.

> and, with a view to the latter object [i.e. 3. above], that no disorder of the mind shall poison his affections, pervert his sense of right, or prevent the exercise of his natural faculties – that no insane delusion shall influence his will in disposing of his property and bring about a disposal of it which, if the mind had been sound, would not have been made.[1]

Who nowadays can match such delicious eloquence? Certainly my wording of the first three tests does not stand comparison and, to cut a long story short, I interpret the fourth test as having a sound and rational mind.

It is also important that a person making a will should not be subject to an undue influence from anyone else. In other words, a testator should be exercising his own free will (i.e. choice), although with due regard to reasonable advice offered to him.

These principles arise from issues relating to wills. It is also appropriate to follow them for other dispositions such as making gifts to people outright or through the medium of a trust.

It is also important to bear in mind that wills and other types of document are subject to strict formalities and that failure to observe them may render the document invalid. It is not mandatory to take legal advice in such matters but it is often prudent to do so, especially where a lot is at stake, as may well be the case with a will.

## powers of attorney

A power of attorney is a legal document that allows someone to appoint another or others to manage his affairs, particularly ones of a financial or business nature. The person making the appointment is the **donor** of the power and a delegate is an **attorney**. A person may wish to create a power if he is going abroad for a period. He would create a **general power** to cover his affairs generally or a **special power** for a particular transaction or limited range of transactions (e.g. the sale of some property).

A person can create a power of attorney only if he has the legal capacity to do so. Subject to exceptions, a power of attorney is revoked automatically if the donor loses legal capacity. In addition, a person cannot be forced to create a power and, similarly, someone else cannot be forced to act as attorney.

---

1  Mark Simeon Jones, 'Testamentary Capacity and the Golden Rule Revisited', *Trust Quarterly Review*, Aug. 2006, 4:3, p. 27.

There are risks with creating a power and a careful choice of attorney is needed. Similarly, there are risks with accepting such an appointment and an attorney is expected to exercise a reasonable level of skill in carrying out his duties.

## enduring powers of attorney

An exception to the rule that powers are revoked by the donor's loss of capacity was introduced in the 1980s in the form of an **enduring power of attorney** (**EPA**). The essence of an EPA is that a person makes it in a prescribed legal format at a time when he has the legal capacity to do so. The power can then be used as an ordinary one but it often lies dormant. An EPA may, like ordinary powers, be general or special but is often general.

When an attorney of an EPA becomes aware that the donor is losing legal capacity, he is under a duty to register the EPA with the Public Guardianship Office (PGO) of the Court of Protection. There is a set procedure that involves giving notice to close relatives of the donor and, when registration is complete, the attorney can handle the donor's affairs in accordance with the terms of the EPA.

Again, an attorney is expected to exercise a reasonable level of skill as well as keeping the donor's money separate from his own, avoiding conflicts of interest between his own affairs and those of the donor and keeping adequate records of transactions carried out for the donor. Decisions that an attorney cannot take on as attorney, however, relate to the donor's personal care or welfare and his health care or treatment.

## lasting powers of attorney

The Mental Capacity Act 2005 introduced, among other things, **lasting powers of attorney** (LPAs) in place of EPAs and the provisions apply from 1 October 2007. EPAs made before the commencement of the act will continue to have effect.

LPAs will enable a donor to delegate decisions over personal care and health care as well as financial ones. It will bring in too a new system of safeguards to protect people who become unable to make decisions for themselves.

## operation of bank accounts

A person may delegate the operation of his bank account in less sophisticated ways while he retains the capacity to conduct his own affairs. One is to arrange for a third party to be a signatory on the account to withdraw money and carry out other transactions. The account-holder needs to make suitable arrangements with the bank or building society.

Another expedient is to place the account in joint names so that the delegate can operate the account as a joint holder. Again, it is a case of making arrangements with the bank or building society.

With either method, the ground rules should be clearly understood and delegation confined to a trusted individual, probably a close relative such as a son or daughter.

Receivership comes into play when a person has significant assets, loses the mental capacity to conduct his own affairs and has not created a valid EPA. In such an instance, it is necessary to appoint a receiver, often a close relative but it may be a friend or a professional such as a solicitor.

The Court of Protection has the power to appoint receivers and administers its jurisdiction through its PGO. The PGO issues guidance on the conditions and method of appointment of a receiver, the receiver's duties and the court fees payable. The role of receiver is akin to that of an attorney or a trustee and is one not to be taken on lightly.

## 13.6 conflicts of interest

This chapter has covered a diverse series of topics, many of which build on earlier parts of the book. Looking after your own affairs can be onerous enough. Helping someone else with theirs can carry heavier responsibilities than dealing with your own and, on occasion, you may encounter a tricky balancing act with regard to the interests of those involved.

If you encounter conflicts of interest, it is important to recognise them for what they are and to manage them promptly and sensitively to avoid family disputes. A person with brothers and sisters who is helping a parent might be well advised to confer with his siblings at an early opportunity. If need be, he should resort to independent advice.

The charity Action on Elder Abuse issued a report on 30 January 2007 on Elder Abuse. Research had revealed a disturbing level of fraud perpetrated by sons and daughters, often in middle age, on their elderly parents (see www. elderabuse.org.uk).

*case study*

This chapter is an attempt to illustrate many of the points made in the earlier ones by means of a hypothetical case study based on the outline biography in Section 1.3 that I now reproduce.

| Phase | Age | Life events | Financial position |
|---|---|---|---|
| 1 | Up to 18 | School education | Reliant on parents and casual earnings for upkeep and pocket money |
| 2 | 19–22 | In higher education | Needs to manage own expenditure<br>Reliant on parental allowance, casual earnings and student debt |
| 3 | 23–30 | Gap year<br>Starts work<br>Moves out from family home<br>Buys own house (on mortgage)<br>Marries (or equivalent)<br>Gets established in career | Poverty followed by reasonable earnings that increase steadily<br>Repayment of student debt<br>Responsibilities and commitments grow<br>Need for long-term provision |
| 4 | 31–40 | Young children<br>Self or partner leaves work temporarily or indefinitely<br>Working parent continues up career ladder | Good income but high commitments<br>Income reduced if one partner not earning |

| 5 | 41–55 | Children become more expensive, especially if in higher education High earnings; both partners working | High earnings and high outgoings May be potential for some savings |
| 6 | 56–65 | Parental responsibilities end Support for elderly parents (mainly practical) Retirement | Earnings peak – plenty of scope for saving Transition to pension Possible inheritance |
| 7 | Over 65 | Retired Plenty of leisure time and travel Own health considerations | Comfortable or well-off Commitments increase if unable to continue in own home |

I have called the subject Chris. Although, in this hypothetical example, Chris is male, all the life phases would be equally applicable to a female. I assume that Chris comes from a typical family in terms of upbringing and means so that he can expect limited financial support only from his parents for higher education and beyond.

I have divided the biography into seven phases and I look at each one in turn. In practice, there is unlikely to be a rigid distinction between the phases, especially beyond phase 2, but they help with dividing the task into manageable bites.

## Phase 1 – school education

| Phase | Age | Life events | Financial position |
|---|---|---|---|
| 1 | Up to 18 | School education | Reliant on parents and casual earnings for upkeep and pocket money |

Phase 1 is essentially life until age 18 on the footing that Chris stays at school until that age. For most if not all of that period, Chris is dependent on his parents for the necessities of life. He takes on some part-time jobs to earn some extra pocket money and build up some resources for higher education, etc.

During his teens especially, Chris learns some basics about handling money, including the concept of budgeting. His parents encourage him to save a proportion of his earnings and arrange for him to open a bank account when he is 16. As part of the arrangement with the bank, he maintains a current account and a deposit account and he can write cheques provided he does not overdraw his current account. He is also allowed a debit card, provided his current account remains in credit, but not a credit card.

He passes his driving test a few months after his 17th birthday but is not yet in a position to buy a car of his own. His parents allow him to drive one of their cars and they meet the cost of the insurance.

Chris has started to become financially aware and to handle the simplest of financial concepts and services. However, his parents have supported and guided him and the next step is to start standing on his own two feet.

## Phase 2 – higher education

| Phase | Age | Life events | Financial position |
|---|---|---|---|
| 2 | 19–22 | Higher education | Needs to manage own expenditure Reliant on parental allowance, casual earnings and student debt |

Higher education is intended primarily in the academic sense. Like many other students, however, Chris goes to university away from home and, during term-time at least, his parents are less accessible. Hence, it is also a time of higher education in life skills including ones relating to personal finance.

An immediate challenge is to manage on his own his day-to-day income and expenditure, particularly the latter. It is quite a big step in that income is relatively scarce and the temptations to spend are great. Fortunately, Chris has become reasonably adept at budgeting and he has talked through the process with his parents before setting pen to paper.

Debts are inevitable at this stage, even though Chris has built up some savings, and he is well aware of the need to keep them to a minimum. Among other things, Chris has decided to try and exist without a credit card, especially as his bank has given him a student account with a modest borrowing facility on favourable terms.

His student loan will need to last him well into the future. He decides to take up what he can and to deposit most of it on a mini cash ISA as the interest earned on it will be greater than the debit interest on his loan. He also finds a part-time job for two evenings a week to supplement his income.

His finances still do not run to a car of his own; if nothing else, the cost of insurance would be prohibitive. He has, however, significant possessions (including a computer) at university that are insured under an extension to his parents' household policy.

At the end of his course, Chris has an outstanding student loan of £13,000. Repayment is not an immediate issue although Chris would like to clear the slate as soon as he reasonably can.

## Phase 3 – getting established

| Phase | Age | Life events | Financial position |
|-------|-----|-------------|--------------------|
| 3 | 23–30 | Gap year | Poverty followed by reasonable |
| | | Starts work | earnings that increase steadily |
| | | Moves out from family | Repayment of student debt |
| | | home | Responsibilities and |
| | | Buys own house (on | commitments grow |
| | | mortgage) | Need for long-term provision |
| | | Marries (or equivalent) | |
| | | Gets established in career | |

Chris has a degree in computer science and has approached a number of ICT firms over employment. He has also considered a gap year but has decided to try to work for a few years and perhaps then take time out on travelling or whatever.

He manages to find a suitable position after a few weeks on a salary that will invoke repayments of his student loan. The location of the job means too that he has finally to move from his parents' home and he shares a rented house to start with. The landlord is responsible for insuring the house but Chris has now to insure his own possessions.

It is time for another budgeting exercise. His major outgoings include his rent, subsistence and repayments on his student loan. He is also keen to start saving for the deposit on a house and is aware of the need to provide for a pension as soon as he reasonably can. He has no dependants at this stage so that life insurance is not an issue.

As to pensions, his employer provides access to a stakeholder personal pension and matches employees' contributions up to 3 per cent of their salaries. Chris decides he can afford his own contributions of 3 per cent and also make monthly contributions to an ISA.

Income tax will now be a consideration. Chris is unlikely to have to complete self-assessment returns for the foreseeable future but he has to ensure that his earnings are declared for tax purposes. In practice, his employer's PAYE is likely to cope with most of the administration.

The next significant event is Chris's engagement to a schoolteacher, Sam. They are both in rented accommodation so decide to buy a house in their joint names. They earn good salaries and have saved sufficient to put down a deposit for a modest property. They borrow the rest on a repayment mortgage.

As a married couple, they decide (sensibly in my opinion) to consider their personal finances on a joint basis from now on. Hence they take out life insurance protection for their mortgage on both their lives; any outstanding balance of the loan will be paid off if either dies.

In the meantime, their salaries are rising steadily so they set aside what they can in savings. They keep some money readily accessible in a deposit account and, for the longer term, build up a spread of unit trusts, OEICs and investment trusts in ISAs to shelter the income and capital profits from tax.

They also keep a wary eye on pension provision. Sam, as a public sector employee, is in a generous final salary scheme although there is still scope for supplementary contributions to a personal plan, including during periods out of work. Chris, on the other hand, has to rely mainly on personal plans and there is greater onus on him to monitor his position carefully.

## Phase 4 – young children

| Phase | Age | Life events | Financial position |
|-------|-----|-------------|--------------------|
| 4 | 31–40 | Young children<br>Self or partner leaves work<br>temporarily or indefinitely<br>Working parent continues<br>up career ladder | Good income but high<br>commitments<br>Income reduced if one<br>partner not earning |

When a couple of children come along, Chris and Sam square up to the implications of early death or of incapacity. Even if the wife had not been earning, the husband would need financial provision to help him look after their young offspring. Such considerations raise the subject of insurance and one line of enquiry is Chris's employer. Provision through a group scheme of a private-sector employer is generally cheaper than arrangements made separately, notwithstanding that an employee has to pay the premiums himself.

Other considerations include wills and the design of benefits under their pension plans to ensure adequate protection for the survivor initially and the children ultimately. For instance, they should both make wills in which, among other things, they can nominate guardians to look after minor children in the event of their both dying prematurely.

Chris and Sam are also interested in private medical insurance. Chris has access to a group scheme operated by his employer but he would have to meet the premiums attributable to him and his family. Hence they have to balance the costs against other commitments and desirables. Even if the premiums are affordable now, annual rises tend to be well above general price inflation, something that they factor into their calculations. They think twice about taking out such cover.

Another serious decision is whether or not the wife returns to work or stays at home to look after the children. Alternatively, the wife might return to work and the husband stay at home. Money is just one consideration but, if either stays at home, the family will suffer a drop in income although it may gain the benefit of child benefit (and, if in straitened circumstances, working and child tax credits).

If, on the other hand, both continue to work, they will need to arrange support for the young children. Some employers provide crèche facilities but charges for professional care normally have to be paid for out of taxed income.

Many parents want to send their children to private schools. Both Chris and Sam realise, however, that their finances are never likely to stretch to ever-escalating school fees for two children and they have sufficient confidence in the standards of the local state schools.

Not overstretching themselves financially also means that they can move to a larger house. They have calculated that they can cope with the greater running costs of the home itself as well as the interest and repayments of a substantially higher mortgage.

Another aspect concerning the children is Child Trust Funds. The childrens' grandparents offer to meet the annual tax-free allowances permitted to supplement the government's contributions.

## Phase 5 – older children

| Phase | Age | Life events | Financial position |
|---|---|---|---|
| 5 | 41–55 | Children become more expensive, especially if in higher education High earnings; both partners working | High earnings and high outgoings May be potential for some savings |

In the event, Sam stayed at home for a few years and then went back to teaching, initially part-time and, when the children were more self-sufficient, full-time. Chris has moved up the scale steadily and their joint incomes comfortably match their commitments, with a bit to spare, by the time the children are in their early teens. The next challenge, however, is higher education and both their children hope to go to university.

Chris is keen to retire by age 60 at the latest and is well aware that the state scheme will fall well short of his financial aspirations and only become available from age 65 at the earliest. Hence, he has increased his contributions to personal plans over the years. Sam paid into a low-cost stakeholder scheme while at home with the children. On top of that, they have built up a reasonable nest egg through regular savings plans, including ISAs, that should help with the children's higher education and with their own retirement.

## Phase 6 – 'empty-nesters'

| Phase | Age | Life events | Financial position |
|---|---|---|---|
| 6 | 56–65 | Parental responsibilities end Support for elderly parents (mainly practical) Retirement | Earnings peak – plenty of scope for saving Transition to pension Possible inheritance |

By the time Chris and Sam are in their mid-50s, their children are self-sufficient, their mortgage is small and their financial commitments are lower than they have ever been. They now enjoy a few years of high earnings during which they can spend reasonably generously on themselves and, at the same time, put away significant sums for the future. They also reap a windfall through a legacy from Sam's maiden aunt.

With their increasing wealth, their minds turn to Inheritance Tax and what they might do to minimise the tax on their estates for the benefit of their children. They realise that IHT planning is closely related to the subject of wills and so they decide to take advice on the steps open to them.

Their parents are now well into their 80s, have been living in their own homes and are financially independent. Chris and Sam are both only children and their parents rely on them heavily for support in business and practical matters. The elderly couples come to accept the constraints of continuing in their own homes and, with Chris and Sam's help, find places in suitable care homes.

Although such matters have limited impact on Chris and Sam's own finances, the commitment in terms of time and emotional strain is significant. On the other hand, they stand to benefit eventually from their parents' estates. As a measure of IHT planning, they ask the parents to consider leaving substantial parts of their estates direct to their own children, thus bypassing Chris and Sam's own estates. The parents grant EPAs to Chris and Sam, largely to meet the contingency that they lose the capacity to handle their own affairs (see Section 13.5), at the same time as they make new wills.

Retirement comes to both Chris and Sam at age 60 whereupon Sam receives a lump sum and starts to draw her teacher's pension. They both have various options over drawing the benefits of their personal plans and, as Chris's has grown to a considerable sum, he decides to take specialist advice on what to do.

They are now in a position to indulge their passion for travel and other pursuits that they have had little time for in the past. They are both sprightly for their early 60s and are able to enjoy the next five years to the hilt.

## Phase 7 – the twilight years

| Phase | Age | Life events | Financial position |
|---|---|---|---|
| 7 | Over 65 | Retired<br>Plenty of leisure time and travel<br>Own health considerations | Comfortable or well-off<br>Commitments increase if unable to continue in own home |

By the time they are 65, their parents have died and Chris and Sam have administered their estates as executors and trustees with some help from a local solicitor. They themselves are comfortably off financially and their children are making their way in life. State pensions kick in but are a bonus rather than a lifeline.

As ever, Chris and Sam plan ahead again in the realisation that they are slowing down physically and would like to unload some of the burdens of managing their own finances. They decide to sell the family home and move to a wardened apartment in a reasonably central location. They also engage the services of a financial manager to look after their investment portfolio.

They now have considerable leisure time and are able to take three or four holidays a year. At the same time, they are starting to creak and investigate taking out private medical insurance (they had decided against doing so hitherto).

I prefer to end the story at this stage. The study has been somewhat idealised to illustrate various points made earlier in the book and I have sidestepped complications such as redundancy and divorce. In addition, it is based on traditional values and the financial wisdom of the early twenty-first century. Goodness only knows what will have replaced them several generations ahead.

looking after your interests

introduction – advice – regulation and standards – what if things turn sour – techniques for handling complaints – information – master of your destiny

## 15.1 introduction

Chapter 1 set the scene for the book by introducing my approach to personal finance, by suggesting ways in which to achieve competence in the subject and by extolling the virtues of having a sense of purpose. Chapter 2 started to tackle the subject itself with a few definitions.

Chapters 3–13 examined specific areas or topics while Chapter 14 sought to draw the threads together by means of a hypothetical case study. The object of this chapter is to help you progress from theory to reality.

Without repeating a lot of detail, a key message I tried to convey in Chapter 1 was the importance of achieving mastery of your own destiny. I advised starting with 'the big picture', i.e. understanding the scope of the subject, and the primary aim of this book is to help you in that respect.

There was also a rough and ready logic to the order of Chapters 3 to 13. Chapter 3 described basic tools while some of the later chapters involved the application of material in earlier ones. Chapter 11 introduced the all-embracing subject of pensions: why all-embracing?

To have a reasonable understanding of pensions, you need also a working knowledge of many other concepts. The idea of saving up for retirement is simple enough. If, however, you are intending to buy a personal pension, the tough bit can be grasping the issues relating to the underlying investments – and the decisions that they entail - rather than the benefits which the plan should provide.

Pensions are a particularly good example of where a broad knowledge of personal finance is helpful even at a tender age (late teens or early 20s). You need to build up a formidable capital sum to provide an adequate income in retirement and there are compelling arguments to start early. Whether you save through a formal pension contract or some other vehicle is another matter.

Employees of employers associated with good occupational schemes are well advised to take advantage of membership if they can. For the self-employed and employees without access to an effective occupational scheme, the way forward is less clear-cut.

I am not suggesting that everyone should start buying a pension by their twenty-third birthday or whatever. What is sensible, however, is that they consider at an early age how they are to provide for their retirement and examine the options open to them. They should then be in a stronger position to make informed decisions over whether or not to start saving for retirement and, if they are to do so soon, over the method that appeals to them most.

A working knowledge of investments is useful if not essential in an exercise of this nature. I made the point in Section 8.6 that the likes of pension plans and ISAs are essentially tax-free wrappers. They are merely methods of holding investments that attract tax advantages. The fundamental issue with both, however, is the choice of underlying investments. Successful investment performance will count for an awful lot in either a pension plan or an ISA.

I have homed in on pensions, ISAs and investments because they are inextricably related. There are various other links, some close and others more tenuous, between the areas of personal finance but it is difficult to recognise and understand them without an insight into the big picture.

The following sections of this chapter apply, in varying degrees, to most if not all areas of personal finance. Appointing a suitable adviser may be more involved than it appears at first sight and is the subject of the next section. Areas of personal finance have become highly regulated over the years so I have introduced some concepts of 'regulation and standards'. I follow with a few hints on what to do if things go wrong and suggest some techniques for handling complaints. Last but not least, I provide some pointers to sources of information.

## 15.2 advice

Few people manage to get through life without having to seek professional advice whether in personal finance or another area. You may be master of your destiny but most of us achieve expert status in relatively few subjects and aspire to 'jack of all trades' beyond that. Even if you do not resort to advice, there may also be occasions when you consider doing so but decide that the potential rewards fail to justify the expense.

It should rarely be necessary to take formal advice with relatively simple products such as bank accounts. It is largely a matter of deciding the features of most importance to you, comparing a range of examples, satisfying yourself on the merits of a particular organisation and getting on with it. A frequent problem in situations of this sort is being spoilt for choice and whittling down a plethora of offerings to a workable shortlist. Surveys published in newspapers and journals and on the Internet can help by cutting down on the legwork.

At the other extreme, wills and trusts involve complex legal documents that a layman attempts to draft at his peril. Besides, documentation is only one aspect. You should thoroughly understand the practical effects of what you intend and approach the tax rules as if you were entering a minefield.

In between, circumstances usually dictate whether or not, and in what respects, you need advice. For instance, you can arrange motor insurance either directly with an insurer or indirectly through the agency of an insurance broker. Similarly, you can deal direct with a bank or building society over a mortgage or go to a mortgage broker or specialist financial adviser for help. There are no hard and fast rules over which method to use, particularly if you are reasonably familiar with what you need and the range of products on offer.

The existence of special circumstances may well warrant the services of an intermediary. This is because the normal run of products is unavailable or unsuitable so that a deeper knowledge of the market is called for. A motorist with a poor driving record or a would-be borrower with a chequered credit history are examples. In such cases, the price (premiums or interest rate) will reflect the extra risk and there will be the added cost of the intermediary's remuneration, often disguised as a commission paid by the product provider. The involvement of an intermediary may, nonetheless, be the difference between finding something affordable and facing complete rejection.

Various 'scandals' over the sale of life assurance and other financial products have peppered the news headlines in recent years. They illustrate the pitfalls to watch out for if you need advice on the investment of money. I have highlighted already the significance of wise investment for personal pensions; you might be talking about a lot of money and a long timespan. The quality of advice is pivotal to achieving good results.

## financial advice

There are many categories of investment adviser and even some firms of solicitors offer advice in this field. With collective schemes such as unit trusts, OIECs and life-assurance policies, however, there is an important generic distinction between **tied** and **independent**.

Tied advisers work for a product supplier and their job is to sell that firm's products. Nonetheless, they have obligations to perform a fact-find ('know your customer') to understand your genuine needs and to offer the most suitable products from their employer's range. If there is nothing suitable in the range, they may refer you elsewhere.

Independent advisers, on the other hand, work for you. Even so, they often have a vested interest in selling you something but they are not limited to a particular product provider. Their task is to ascertain your needs and then to suggest the best product that is available to meet them.

Somewhere between are **multi-tied** advisers. They are affiliated to a number of product providers but, apart from that, they are tied rather than independent.

## the remuneration of financial advisers

Professional advisers have to earn a living like everyone else. I have no objection to that, provided they carry out their jobs diligently and honestly. Even so, it can help to understand how their bread is buttered, i.e. what they themselves stand to gain from a transaction.

Financial advisers can be paid in either of two main ways that I call **direct** and **indirect**. The direct method is to charge a fee to their customer or client ('principal'). They generally base their fees on an hourly rate so that if, for example, they undertake three hours' work at £100 an hour, the bill comes to £300 (plus VAT). The indirect method is a commission, or something equivalent, from the firm whose products the adviser sells. In this case, the adviser does not submit a bill to his principal but is paid behind the scenes, so to speak. For example, if the adviser introduces business in the form of an investment of £20,000 in a unit trust, he may receive a commission from the unit trust management company of 3 per cent, which amounts, in this case, to £600 (£20,000 × 3/100).

When dealing with a financial adviser, it is important to establish at the outset the terms of business and, in particular, the method and rate of remuneration. An adviser must offer a choice between fees and commission as a condition of describing himself as independent.

There are advantages and disadvantages with the respective methods. With commission, the process may appear relatively painless but the impact on the sum actually invested can mount up. Also, an adviser has an incentive to prefer the products that earn him the greatest level of commission.

With fees, the figures are more transparent, although you have the discomfort of writing another cheque. More significantly, however, there should be less temptation for the adviser to promote product A – that maximises the benefit to him – to the exclusion of product B – that would be more suitable for you. The providers of some potentially suitable products pay little or no commission so an arrangement with a fee-based adviser that takes into account commission earnings reduces the danger of skewed recommendations.

The Financial Services Authority announced in February 2007 that it was initiating a review into retail distribution that would incorporate the effect of 'incentives' on the quality of advice. Its discussion paper published on 27 June 2007 heralded reforms 'to address the root causes of persistent problems in the retail investment market'.

## conflicts of interest

The point over commission heralds the subject of conflicts of interest generally. A conflict occurs when the agent stands to benefit personally at the expense of his principal. Advisers and other agents have a legal duty to avoid conflicts of interest or at least to put principals on notice of a potential conflict. Remuneration in cash or in kind is just one way in which conflicts may arise.

In a similar vein, you should understand for whom an adviser is acting. For example, an estate agent is normally the agent for the vendor of a property and not for a purchaser. Hence the agent's primary duty is to the person selling although he has obligations to a potential purchaser over matters such as accuracy of information.

### finding an adviser

How do you set about finding a suitable adviser? As with many things, there are no set rules but I suggest a few pointers.

First, understand and define the issue that you are faced with. For example, you may have sufficient earnings from which to set aside significant monthly savings. How should you invest your savings? Should it be in bank deposits, life assurance policies, ISAs or a personal pension plan? Maybe you need more general financial advice before drilling down to a specific such as a pension plan.

Second, identify the categories of adviser whom you might consult. Sometimes the range is pretty obvious; for example, you want a lawyer to draft a property lease or a stockbroker to buy shares. Increasingly, however, the traditional boundaries between disciplines are becoming blurred as organisations extend their ranges of services.

Life within traditional boundaries is also becoming more complicated in that individual practices concentrate on narrow areas of business. Thus, if you have a concern over personal pensions, one avenue is a financial adviser who specialises in pensions work. The rules of the industry regulator, the Financial Services Authority, require certain types of financial adviser to have specific qualifications such as in relation to pensions or mortgage business.

Third. take some trouble over selecting an adviser of the appropriate type. Again, there are various ways to set about the task. One is to obtain a list of affiliated firms or practitioners from a professional organisation (see also Further reading and resources). Even so, a list of names does not tell you how effective the candidates are in practice and who will be most suitable for you A personal recommendation from a trusted contact is another line of enquiry. Also, financial advisers must supply key facts documents about their services and costs.

Once you have made a possible choice, ask for an exploratory meeting on a 'no commitment' basis to meet the individual you would be dealing with, to ask about his qualifications and experience and to ascertain other relevant matters such as charges, the treatment of clients' money and other business methods. References from existing clients are another consideration, especially if you are working from a list or directory. A written contract or letter of engagement should set out the rights and obligations of both parties and you can ask to see one in draft.

## 15.3 regulation and standards

### Financial Services Authority

Most firms and practitioners conducting business in the realm of personal finance are regulated to a greater or lesser degree. The point is particularly true of banking, life assurance, insurance and all aspects of investment. The principal regulator is the FSA and I am sympathetic to remarks implying that financial services regulation is becoming an industry in its own right.

Even so, regulation is not a panacea for everything and consumers are expected to take a reasonable level of responsibility for their own actions. Copious rules and regulations are designed to set acceptable standards for the industry and, if a firm can demonstrate that it has acted in accordance with the law, it is difficult for an aggrieved consumer to press home a complaint.

## Financial Services Ombudsman

A body that rejoices in the title of Financial Services Ombudsman handles customer complaints. In addition, firms are required to maintain their own procedures and a customer may resort to the Ombudsman only after he has gone through all stages of a firm's internal scheme.

## Financial Services Compensation Scheme

The Financial Services Compensation Scheme provides compensation for financial loss arising from a bank, building society, insurance company or other firm engaged in 'regulated business' becoming unable to meet its obligations. The amount of compensation varies according to the nature of the business and is for financial loss only (not, for example, for 'stress and suffering'). Generally, however, entitlement may be limited to a specified ceiling and a proportion of the loss suffered. There are also conditions to be satisfied.

The maximum levels of compensation per person, per firm and per type of business as at early 2007 are:

| | |
|---|---|
| Bank and building society deposits | 100% of first £2,000<br>90% of next £33,000<br>Maximum £31,700 |
| 1. Investments<br>2. Mortgage advice and arranging | 100% of first £30,000<br>90% of next £20,000<br>Maximum £48,000 |
| Long-term insurance<br>(pensions and life) | 100% of first £2,000 of valid claims<br>90% of remainder (no maximum) |
| Compulsory general insurance<br>(e.g. motor third-party) | 100% of valid claims<br>(no maximum) |
| Non-compulsory general insurance<br>(e.g. household) | 100% of first £2,000 of valid claims<br>90% of remainder (no maximum) |

## CAT standards and Stakeholder standards

CAT and **Stakeholder** are standards set by the government as benchmarks to help consumers compare financial products that fall within certain categories.

It is important to understand, however, that the standards are not guarantees of performance or risk. In addition, a product that conforms to CAT or Stakeholder standards is not necessarily better than an equivalent one that does not.

CAT stands for charges, access and terms. CAT standards only apply now to mortgages and there are two sets, one for loans with a variable rate of interest and the other for loans starting with a fixed or capped rate of interest.

Stakeholder standards relate to deposit accounts (within or outside a mini cash ISA), certain collective investments (that can be held within or outside an ISA), personal pensions and CTFs. An important feature for investment-related products is a maximum level of charges.

The standards are reproduced in full on the FSA's website (see also Further reading and resources).

## key features

The providers of unit trusts, OEICS, life assurance bonds and other financial products are required to supply key features documents to private investors. The documents explain how the products work, the main risks, the charges and other information that an investor might be interested in. They are generally written in modern English and, while not exciting, they are comprehensive and readable.

## consumer credit

The Consumer Credit Act 1974 set up a system of licensing for anyone engaged in consumer credit business (as defined in the legislation) with individuals. The Act's other aims include (i) regulation of the formation, terms and enforcement of credit and equivalent agreements and (ii) truth in lending through requirements to show the true cost of credit. The Consumer Credit Act 2006 aims to enhance the protection of borrowers and the government is implementing its provisions in stages.

The Government's Office of Fair Trading administers the system of licensing and, with the courts, has duties over enforcement of the Acts. A lender who fails to comply may have difficulty in recovering money he has advanced. There is currently an upper limit of £25,000 on 'consumer credit agreements' covered by the legislation but the limit is to be removed from 6 April 2008 for new borrowing (see www. berr.gov.uk formerly www.dti.gov.uk).

Section 75 of the Consumer Credit Act Credit 1974 is worth knowing about in relation to credit card transactions of £100 or more. The benefit of the section is best illustrated by an example. You buy a washing machine for £350 from an electrical store and pay by credit card. After a month, the machine breaks down and, by virtue of Section 75, you have a claim against the credit card company as well as the store for the defective goods.

## other regulators

There are various regulatory bodies associated with occupational pensions including the Pensions Regulator, the Pensions Ombudsman (for complaints) and the Pensions Protection Fund (particularly relevant for members of final-salary schemes when an employer company is unable to meet its obligations).

The Law Society is the regulator for practising solicitors and operates a service for consumer complaints. The government has plans, however, to transfer the complaints function to an independent Legal Services Ombudsman.

The Ombudsman for Estate Agents provides an independent complaints service for buyers and sellers of residential property in the UK.

## codes of practice

A code of practice is generally a form of voluntary regulation adopted by members of an industry or association. An important example is the Banking Code entered into by banks, building societies, credit card companies and National Savings & Investments applicable to personal customers. The subscribers promise to meet a set of commitments and standards relating to banking services. You can find further information, including the full code, on the British Bankers' Association website www.bba.org.uk.

## 15.4 what if things turn sour?

Diligent investigations before the appointment of an adviser reduce the risk of things going wrong later but by no means eliminate it. You should always exercise vigilance in matters of business although the distinction between reasonable trust and undue suspicion may be blurred. Professionals expect clients to be on their mettle but an apparent lack of respect can be highly demotivating.

Try to avoid dealing with an organisation, especially one with direct control over your assets, if there is any hint of it leaving you high and dry in the foreseeable future. Schemes such as the Financial Services Compensation Scheme may provide a cushion if things go badly wrong but regard them as no more than that.

The regulatory complaints schemes supplement rather than displace a consumer's remedies under the general laws of tort, contract, etc. They usually have the attractions of greater accessibility and negligible risk over costs so that you should at least consider the relevant one if the need arises. There are, however, limitations on the grievances you may pursue and on the levels of compensation that an ombudsman may award.

Refusal of credit facilities can cause frustration and embarrassment, especially if you are ignorant of the reason for being turned down. A lender is under no obligation to explain his reasons although I would be disappointed at total silence. More specifically, try asking the lender if he has used information supplied by a credit reference agency and, if so, which one. You can then ask the agency, on submission of the relevant details and payment of a small fee, for a copy of your file to check if the information is correct. If need be, inform the agency of any corrections with evidence to support them.

If, on the other hand, you are in debt but unable to meet your obligations, possible sources of help and advice include the National Debtline, the Consumer

Credit Counselling Service and local Citizens Advice Bureaux. There are further details in Further reading and resources.

## 15.5 techniques for handling complaints

Making a complaint, especially a formal one, can involve inordinate stress and expenditure of time and energy. Regrettably, I am speaking from experience and I strongly recommend trying to resolve an issue in its early stages. A diplomatic telephone call and a little 'give and take' may avoid hours of sweat and anguish. Sort the thing out amicably if you possibly can before positions become entrenched.

If, nonetheless, it is necessary to pursue a complaint, my preferred method is by letter rather than telephone call or e-mail. I have written numerous letters of complaint over the years and I get a curious satisfaction out of succeeding in my cause! There is an art to writing letters in general but an even greater art to writing letters of complaint in particular. Credibility is important and I offer the following suggestions in relation to technique.

▸ Get the fundamentals of letter-writing right. Pay attention to the details of spelling, grammar, form and so on. Type is easier to read than handwriting.
▸ Be clear about your cause of complaint and in a position to justify it. Ask yourself if the matter would stand up in court.
▸ Follow the right channels. If need be, indicate to the firm your intention to lodge a formal complaint and ask about their internal procedures for handling it. The firm should also let you have details in writing about the industry ombudsman scheme where one exists. Avoid unnecessary delay and observe all legitimate deadlines.
▸ Describe clearly your cause for complaint and, if there is a quantifiable loss, produce figures to support your assertions.
▸ Include in your initial letter a succinct and logical narrative of the material facts and circumstances. A reader may be unfamiliar with your case and will wish to build up a mental picture quickly and easily.
▸ Avoid undue paper. If you need to incorporate copies of supporting correspondence or documents, keep them to a minimum and cross-refer.
▸ Choose your words carefully. Your letter should be businesslike and not a whinge. Be factual and avoid aggression and undue emotion. Think carefully about threats; you should be able to back them up with positive action. At the same time, be firm and persistent.
▸ If you remain dissatisfied after exhausting all stages of the internal procedures, establish with the firm that there is deadlock and that it is open to you to refer the matter to the ombudsman (or whatever). An ombudsman will wish to establish the point at the outset.

I hope you never find yourself in this position but, if you do, proceed steadily and keep your eye on the ball.

## 15.6 information

In many respects, your own competence is your most potent weapon and your soundest defence. I expressed the opinion in Section 1.2 that competence is built on knowledge and skill. Skill is developed through proficiency at putting your knowledge into practice. Your knowledge comes from information, so that sources of information are a key ingredient in attaining competence.

There are numerous sources of information that can bewilder as well as inform. As with climbing a ladder, you need to know how to take the first step as that leads to the second, the second to the third, and so on. My emphasis on 'the big picture' is to encourage a broad understanding of the entire subject so that you can work out more easily how individual pieces fit within the jigsaw puzzle and how to set about a complicated issue.

The FSA has four statutory objectives as industry regulator. Three are maintaining market confidence, securing appropriate protection for consumers and fighting financial crime. The fourth and most significant for my purposes is promoting public understanding of the financial system. The four objectives are regarded by Parliament as equals but, to my way of thinking, an understanding of what you are about is tantamount to being your own industry watchdog.

The principal information sources that I use include books, journals, newspapers and websites. To these I should add leaflets, notably ones issued by government departments, regulatory bodies such as the FSA, and charities whose activities impinge on personal finance. The quantity is great and the quality can be mixed. The art of using all these sources of information is to sift out what is really useful and to focus your attention on it.

Further reading and resources lists the material that I have found useful and that I think will be helpful to you. It is by no means exhaustive and, with the Internet in particular, the process of change is awesome. If I can guide you to the first rung of the ladder, perhaps you will be able to find the second yourself, then the third, and so on. I wish you every success in your climb.

## 15.7 master of your destiny

Well, I have said my piece and, if it is of any help to you, the satisfaction is mine. I hope that I have dug a foundation on which you can build your own structure of knowledge and skills.

I have dispensed enough advice but, as a parting shot, I urge you to keep learning. It is a vast subject; you cannot hope to master it all at once and, in any event, it is subject to frequent changes.

analysis of income and expenditure

## general

1 The analysis is for a hypothetical married couple, H being the husband and W the wife.

2 It comprises two sheets of a computer spreadsheet, the first being the principal sheet and the second the supporting sheet showing a breakdown of the expenditure. They have embedded arithemetical functions so that the spreadsheet does the calculations.

3 The analysis is suitable for compiling a budget and for monitoring. I concentrate for this purpose on the monitoring function.

4 H and W have a bank current account in their joint names through which they pass their household income and expenditure. They also have an interest-bearing deposit account and make frequent transfers between the current and deposit accounts with a view to maintaining a sensible working balance on the current account.

5 They have a credit card that they use for occasional payments. They always pay off balances on the credit card account from their bank account before interest starts to run. They show the entries in their spreadsheet when they clear the credit card account from the bank account.

6 Generally, they make entries on a receipts and payments basis, i.e. in the months when the items actually pass through the account.

7 The analysis is for the year 1 April year n to 31 March year n+1 and is divided into months with a total for the entire year of account. They receive monthly statements from their bank and complete the spreadsheets monthly for monitoring purposes.

8 The spreadsheet shows calculated minus (–) amounts automatically.

## principal sheet

1 It is divided into sections for:
  ‣ regular income

- regular expenditure (shown in detail on the supporting sheet with the totals embedded)
- regular income less expenditure – i.e. an arithmetical surplus (or deficit)
- regular savings – contributions to savings or investment schemes out of their surplus income
- balance for the month – the surplus income less the regular savings
- reconciliation – to show the overall movement on their bank current account during the month

2  Regular income: they both work and they have their salaries (net of PAYE, NICs and any other deductions) paid into the account. They also have, as mentioned, an interest-bearing deposit account and own other investments: the income from these assets is directed to the current account. Tax paid is shown as – and tax refunded as +.

3  Irregular items: they are separated from regular income and expenditure and include capital transactions such as (i) transfers to or from deposit and (ii) purchases or sales of investments not regarded as regular savings.

4  They could add, as memorandum items, the balances at the end of a month of the deposit account (credit balance) and credit card account (debit balance if not nil).

## secondary sheet

1  They have divided it into their main categories of expenditure.
2  Items paid by direct debit or standing order are at the start of the analysis and entries they initiate themselves (by debit card, cheque, etc) follow below the subtotal.
3  The column totals are embedded in the regular expenditure section of the principal sheet.

Monthly receipts and payments for year 1 April 2006 to 31 March 2007

| | April | May | June | July | August | September | October | November | December | January | February | March | Total |
|---|---|---|---|---|---|---|---|---|---|---|---|---|---|
| *Regular income:* | | | | | | | | | | | | | |
| H's salary, etc (net) | 2,264.00 | 2,495.38 | 2,479.69 | 2,479.69 | 2,479.69 | 2,717.29 | 2,519.29 | 2,519.29 | 3,519.29 | 2,519.29 | 2,519.29 | 2,519.29 | 31,031.48 |
| W's salary, etc (net) | 957.42 | 969.61 | 974.27 | 974.07 | 1,003.75 | 974.05 | 974.29 | 1,474.06 | 1,071.77 | 1,041.15 | 1,041.25 | 1,045.93 | 12,501.62 |
| Deposit interest | | 140.47 | | 150.98 | | | | 160.42 | | | 170.35 | | 622.22 |
| Securities income | 107.00 | 326.05 | 3,137.12 | 283.65 | 386.66 | 96.81 | 2,514.94 | 409.47 | 19.82 | 315.96 | 313.02 | 17.80 | 7,928.30 |
| Income tax | | | –479.00 | | | | | | | –498.00 | | | –977.00 |
| Totals | 3,328.42 | 3,931.51 | 6,112.08 | 3,737.41 | 4,021.08 | 3,788.15 | 6,008.52 | 4,563.24 | 4,610.88 | 3,378.40 | 4,043.91 | 3,583.02 | 51,106.62 |
| *Regular expenditure:* | | | | | | | | | | | | | |
| (see separate sheet) | 2,195.91 | 1,479.32 | 1,828.65 | 1,641.28 | 4,387.53 | 3,207.68 | 1,657.49 | 2,895.98 | 1,666.47 | 1,733.03 | 3,882.58 | 2,451.06 | 29,026.98 |
| *Regular income – regular expenditure* | 1,132.51 | 2,452.19 | 4,283.43 | 2,096.13 | –366.45 | 580.47 | 4,351.03 | 1,667.26 | 2,944.41 | 1,645.37 | 161.33 | 1,131.96 | 22,079.64 |
| *Regular savings:* | | | | | | | | | | | | | |
| Stakeholder pen. (W) | 234.00 | 234.00 | 234.00 | 234.00 | 234.00 | 234.00 | 234.00 | 234.00 | 234.00 | 234.00 | 234.00 | 234.00 | 2,808.00 |
| ISAs (H and W) | 3,000.00 | 1,000.00 | 1,000.00 | 1,000.00 | 1,000.00 | 1,000.00 | 1,000.00 | 1,000.00 | 1,000.00 | 1,000.00 | 1,000.00 | 1,000.00 | 14,000.00 |
| Totals | 3,234.00 | 1,234.00 | 1,234.00 | 1,234.00 | 1,234.00 | 1,234.00 | 1,234.00 | 1,234.00 | 1,234.00 | 1,234.00 | 1,234.00 | 1,234.00 | 16,808.00 |
| *Balance for month* | –2,101.49 | 1,218.19 | 3,049.43 | 862.13 | –1,600.45 | –653.53 | 3,117.03 | 433.26 | 1,710.41 | 411.37 | –1,072.67 | –102.04 | 5,271.64 |
| *Reconciliation:* | | | | | | | | | | | | | |
| Bank – start | 518.86 | 517.37 | 535.56 | 584.99 | 447.12 | 646.67 | 493.14 | 510.17 | 443.43 | 653.84 | 665.21 | 392.54 | |
| Balance for month | –2,101.49 | 1,218.19 | 3,049.43 | 862.13 | –1,600.45 | –653.53 | 3,117.03 | 433.26 | 1,710.41 | 411.37 | –1,072.67 | –102.04 | |
| Plus irregular credits | 2,100.00 | | | | 10,000.00 | 500.00 | 3,000.00 | 3,000.00 | 1,500.00 | | 800.00 | 200.00 | |
| Minus irregular debits | | 1,200.00 | 3,000.00 | 1,000.00 | 8,200.00 | | 3,100.00 | 3,500.00 | 1,500.00 | 400.00 | | | |
| Bank – end | 517.37 | 535.56 | 584.99 | 447.12 | 646.67 | 493.14 | 510.17 | 443.43 | 653.84 | 665.21 | 392.54 | 490.50 | |

*Note:*
Can include also
deposit a/c – end (cr)
credit card – end (dr)

Regular expenditure

| | April | May | June | July | August | September | October | November | December | January | February | March | Total |
|---|---|---|---|---|---|---|---|---|---|---|---|---|---|
| *Direct debits/standing orders:* | | | | | | | | | | | | | |
| Council tax | 161.10 | 161.00 | 161.00 | 161.00 | 161.00 | 161.00 | 161.00 | 161.00 | 161.00 | 161.00 | | | 1,610.10 |
| Water | 16.50 | 16.50 | 16.50 | 16.50 | 16.50 | 16.50 | 16.50 | 16.50 | 16.50 | 16.50 | 16.50 | 21.90 | 203.40 |
| Gas | 44.00 | 44.00 | 44.00 | 44.00 | 44.00 | 44.00 | 49.00 | 49.00 | 49.00 | 49.00 | 49.00 | 49.00 | 558.00 |
| Electricity | 21.00 | 21.00 | 21.00 | 21.00 | 21.00 | 21.00 | 24.00 | 24.00 | 24.00 | 24.00 | 24.00 | 24.00 | 270.00 |
| Telephone | 23.00 | 23.00 | 23.00 | 23.00 | 23.00 | 23.00 | 23.00 | 23.00 | 23.00 | 24.00 | 24.00 | 24.00 | 279.00 |
| Service contract | 28.20 | 28.20 | 28.20 | 28.20 | 28.20 | | | 30.50 | 30.50 | 30.50 | 30.50 | 30.50 | 293.50 |
| House insurance | 40.43 | 40.43 | 40.43 | 40.43 | 40.43 | 40.43 | 40.43 | 42.15 | 42.15 | 42.15 | 42.15 | 77.70 | 529.31 |
| Motor insurance | | | | | | | | 310.50 | | | | | 310.50 |
| Other insurance | | | | | | | | 15.99 | | | | | 15.99 |
| TV licence | | | | | | | 126.50 | | | | | | 126.50 |
| Mortgage payments | 352.75 | 352.75 | 352.75 | 352.75 | 352.75 | 380.40 | 380.40 | 380.40 | 380.40 | 380.40 | 380.40 | 380.40 | 4,426.55 |
| Life-assurance premiums | 135.90 | 135.90 | 135.90 | 135.90 | 135.90 | 135.90 | 135.90 | 135.90 | 135.90 | 135.90 | 135.90 | 135.90 | 1,630.80 |
| *Subtotals* | 822.88 | 822.78 | 822.78 | 822.78 | 822.78 | 822.23 | 956.73 | 1,188.94 | 862.45 | 863.45 | 702.45 | 743.40 | 10,253.65 |
| *Other:* | | | | | | | | | | | | | |
| Routine household | 264.80 | 222.24 | 267.35 | 263.35 | 263.94 | 259.51 | 239.30 | 332.88 | 441.69 | 247.89 | 283.95 | 196.85 | 3,283.75 |
| House maintenance and equipment | 73.45 | 20.65 | 148.62 | | 99.96 | 42.88 | | 27.79 | | 14.42 | 2,095.32 | 80.29 | 2,603.38 |
| Motor car maintenance | | 18.80 | | 58.00 | | | 115.00 | 358.03 | | | | 10.05 | 559.88 |
| Motor car fuel | 98.29 | 42.16 | 62.83 | 75.06 | 48.00 | 70.07 | 40.01 | 45.67 | 20.00 | 39.00 | 64.00 | 58.00 | 663.09 |
| Holidays | 283.65 | 46.44 | | | 2,608.00 | 1,215.23 | | 308.30 | | | | 309.36 | 4,770.98 |
| Clothes, hair, etc | 61.48 | 57.00 | 12.99 | 96.00 | 86.49 | 253.44 | 22.00 | | 22.00 | 9.50 | 63.50 | 414.00 | 1,098.40 |
| Health | 117.50 | | 30.00 | 55.00 | | 89.60 | | 22.57 | | 60.14 | 19.28 | 235.00 | 629.09 |
| Leisure | 35.95 | 84.50 | 25.60 | 38.90 | 43.90 | 102.77 | 21.00 | 19.50 | 84.75 | 24.90 | 119.60 | 18.40 | 619.77 |
| Interests | 117.95 | 57.25 | 103.92 | 78.99 | 26.26 | 155.45 | 30.95 | 75.87 | 38.21 | 259.88 | 133.78 | 63.96 | 1,142.47 |
| Subscriptions | | 25.00 | 99.50 | | | 14.00 | | 16.00 | | 57.00 | 55.00 | 132.00 | 398.50 |
| Charity-giving | 30.00 | 30.00 | 80.00 | 30.00 | 130.00 | 30.00 | 80.00 | 30.00 | 30.00 | 80.00 | 75.00 | 30.00 | 655.00 |
| Presents | 64.98 | | 48.56 | | 35.00 | 50.00 | | 317.93 | 46.67 | 6.15 | | 39.00 | 608.29 |
| Other | 44.98 | 2.50 | 26.50 | 23.20 | 23.20 | 2.50 | 2.50 | 2.50 | 20.70 | 20.70 | 20.70 | -4.25 | 185.73 |
| Cash withdrawals | 180.00 | 50.00 | 100.00 | 100.00 | 200.00 | 100.00 | 150.00 | 150.00 | 100.00 | 50.00 | 250.00 | 125.00 | 1,555.00 |
| *Totals* | 2,195.91 | 1,479.32 | 1,828.65 | 1,641.28 | 4,387.53 | 3,207.68 | 1,657.49 | 2,895.98 | 1,666.47 | 1,733.03 | 3,882.58 | 2,451.06 | 29,026.98 |

appendix **B**

some mortgage types

| | |
|---|---|
| Repayment | The borrower's regular payments to the lender (usually monthly) pay the interest and repay the capital over the term of the mortgage (often 25 years or more) |
| | If the interest rate is variable, the borrower adjusts the interest element (and hence the regular payments) on changes in the rate |
| | The interest element tends to reduce and the capital element to increase over the term |
| Interest-only | Capital repayment only falls due at the end of the term |
| | The borrower looks to some other savings vehicle, e.g. an endowment policy, to repay the capital |
| Group | Up to four individuals borrow to purchase a property jointly and share the repayments |
| Guarantor | A parent or guardian agrees to cover the repayments if the borrower fails to do so |
| Standard variable rate (SVR) | Lenders have a SVR that is expressed as a margin over an independent base rate (e.g. Bank of England base rate) |
| | Margins are typically 1.5 per cent to 3.5 per cent over the base rate |
| | SVRs are often a lender's most expensive option |
| Discounted | Variable rate mortgages that offer a discount on the lender's SVR for a set period |
| | Revert to SVR at the end of the period |

| | |
|---|---|
| Fixed-rate | The interest rate is fixed for a given period of years before reverting to a lender's SVR |
| Tracker | Variable rate mortgages that follow an independent base rate at a specified differential, e.g. Bank of England base rate + 1 per cent |
| | May revert to SVR after a specified term of years |
| Capped-rate | Variable rate mortgages under which the interest rate rises no higher than a set limit (i.e. the cap) |
| Flexible | Mortgages that allow some flexibility over capital repayments within defined limits |
| | Flexible payments may be above or below the norm or allow skipping of payments |
| Current account Offset | Allow the borrower to take account of savings for calculating the interest on the loan |
| | The interest is generally applied to the net balance (i.e. the excess of the loan over the savings) where separate accounts are involved |
| | Interest rate tends to be slightly higher than for conventional mortgages |
| Endowment | An interest-only mortgage where an endowment policy is earmarked for repayment of the loan |
| | The policy is usually with-profits and written to mature when repayment of the loan falls due |
| Pension | Similar in concept to an endowment mortgage except that the repayment vehicle is a personal pension plan |
| | Only a lump sum commutation payment (up to one-quarter of the policy value) is suitable for repayment of the loan |
| | Particular care is needed with arrangements of this sort |

# redemption yield

I introduced in Section 8.8 the concept of redemption yield and examined it in the context of an imaginary government stock 3% Treasury 2016 redeemable at par on 31 December 2016, ten years from 31 December 2006 when the stock was quoted at 88. The estimated gross redemption yield (GRY) that I calculated was 4.77 per cent.

Another way of looking at the value of a redeemable fixed-interest stock such as a gilt is as a 'stream' of future cash flows generated by it. In this instance, a holder to 31 December 2016 will receive (i) interest at 3 per cent on the nominal value for each of the ten years plus (ii) repayment of the capital in ten years time.

Gilts normally pay interest in two half-yearly instalments but, for simplicity, I assume one annual payment in arrears on 31 December.

The formula for working out the fair value of the cash streams is:

$$P = c/(1 + i) + c/(1 + i)^2 + ..... + c/(1 + i)^n + R/(1 + i)^n$$

where:

P is the present value of the stock (the 'unknown' in the equation)
c is the coupon (i.e. the interest rate of 3 per cent)
R is the redemption proceeds (i.e. the par value of 100)
n is the number of years to redemption (10 in this instance)
i is the rate of interest for discounting the time lag on the cash receipts (I adopt 4.50 per cent).

The formula translates into:

$$P = 3/1.045 + 3/1.045^2 + ..... + 3/1.045^{10} + 100/1.045^{10} = 88.07$$

that is close to my hypothetical price quotation of 88. The discount rate equates to an accurate GRY of 4.50 per cent against my simplified 4.77 per cent. Feeding a discount rate of 4.77 per cent into the formula gives a present value of 86.18 that differs by about 2 per cent from the specified 88.

*Note*: I am grateful to Dr James Mallon of Napier University, Edinburgh for supplying me with the formula.

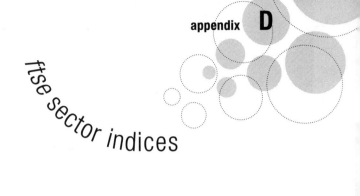

ftse sector indices

Below are the FTSE sector indices as at close of business on 29 December 2006.

The FTSE divides the main market into industries and subdivides them into sectors.

| Industry | Sector | Number of Companies in sector index | Dividend yield (%) for the sector | Dividend cover (x) for the sector | Price/ earnings ratio for the sector |
|---|---|---|---|---|---|
| Oil & Gas | Oil & Gas producers | 14 | 3.17 | 3.09 | 10.20 |
| | Oil Equipment & Services | 6 | 0.96 | 2.65 | 39.24 |
| Basic Materials | Chemicals | 7 | 2.06 | 2.44 | 19.95 |
| | Forestry & Paper | 0 | | | |
| | Industrial Metals | 1 | 1.41 | 4.25 | 16.63 |
| | Mining | 13 | 1.62 | 6.32 | 9.75 |
| Industrials | Construction & Materials | 15 | 2.20 | 2.42 | 18.73 |
| | Aerospace & Defence | 11 | 2.26 | 2.62 | 16.88 |
| | General Industrials | 6 | 3.66 | 1.98 | 13.85 |
| | Electronic & Electrical Equipment | 14 | 1.59 | 3.03 | 20.76 |
| | Industrial Engineering | 18 | 2.30 | 2.48 | 17.48 |
| | Industrial Transportation | 12 | 3.00 | 1.28 | 26.12 |
| | Support Services | 70 | 1.91 | 2.05 | 25.58 |

| Industry | Sector | Number of Companies in sector index | Dividend yield (%) for the sector | Dividend cover (x) for the sector | Price/ earnings ratio for the sector |
|---|---|---|---|---|---|
| Consumer Goods | Automobiles & Parts | 2 | 4.50 | 1.55 | 14.31 |
| | Beverages | 5 | 2.83 | 2.04 | 17.36 |
| | Food Producers | 15 | 2.95 | 3.31 | 10.24 |
| | Household Goods | 14 | 2.02 | 3.17 | 15.59 |
| | Leisure Goods | 6 | 2.94 | N/a | N/a |
| | Personal Goods | 4 | 1.53 | 2.24 | 29.15 |
| | Tobacco | 3 | 3.16 | 1.94 | 16.32 |
| Health Care | Health Care Equipment & Services | 13 | 0.92 | 3.77 | 28.81 |
| | Pharmaceuticals & Biotechnology | 19 | 2.95 | 2.23 | 15.21 |
| Consumer Services | Food & Drug Retailers | 6 | 2.25 | 1.59 | 28.04 |
| | General Retailers | 39 | 2.43 | 1.69 | 24.38 |
| | Media | 34 | 2.31 | 2.09 | 20.76 |
| | Travel & Leisure | 34 | 1.98 | 3.06 | 16.46 |
| Telecomunications | Fixed Line Telecommunications | 7 | 3.67 | 1.69 | 16.12 |
| | Mobile Telecommunications | 2 | 4.28 | 0.90 | 25.88 |
| Utilities | Electricity | 5 | 2.10 | 3.21 | 14.86 |
| | Gas Water & Multiutilties | 7 | 3.64 | 1.27 | 21.60 |
| Financials | Banks | 9 | 4.14 | 1.94 | 12.42 |
| | Nonlife Insurance | 17 | 3.01 | 1.75 | 19.00 |
| | Life Insurance/ Assurance | 9 | 2.86 | 2.14 | 16.35 |
| | Real Estate | 52 | 1.61 | 6.85 | 9.05 |
| | General Financial | 36 | 1.85 | 3.27 | 16.52 |
| | Equity Investment Instruments | 132 | 1.37 | 1.51 | 48.36 |

| Industry | Sector | Number of Companies in sector index | Dividend yield (%) for the sector | Dividend cover (x) for the sector | Price/ earnings ratio for the sector |
|---|---|---|---|---|---|
| Technology | Software & Computer Services | 27 | 1.43 | 2.37 | 29.49 |
| | Technology Hardware & Equipment | 9 | 0.43 | 16.11 | 14.40 |

© FTSE International Limited and *The Financial Times* Limited 2006. All rights reserved. Extracted from the *FT*, 30 December/31 December 2006.

*Note*: There are periodic revisions to the classification.

appendix **E**

*the pensions* commission

Extracts from the First Report of October 2004, Executive Summary (Crown Copyright)

## the demographic challenge and unavoidable choices

Life expectancy is increasing rapidly and will continue to do so. This is good news. But combined with a forecast low birth rate this will produce a near doubling in the percentage of the population aged 65 years and over between now and 2050, with further increase thereafter. The baby boom has delayed the effect of underlying long-term trends, but will now produce 30 years of a very rapid increase in the dependency ratio. We must now make adjustments to public policy and/or individual behaviour which ideally should have been started 20–30 years ago.

Faced with the increasing proportion of the population aged over 65, society and individuals must choose between four options. Either:

(i)   Pensioners will become poorer relative to the rest of society; or
(ii)  taxes/National Insurance Contributions devoted to pensions must rise; or
(iii) savings must rise; or
(iv)  average retirement ages must rise.

But the first option (poorer pensioners) appears unattractive; and there are significant barriers to solving the problem through any one of the other three options alone. Some mix of higher taxes/National Insurance Contributions, higher savings and later average retirement is therefore required.

## average retirement ages: past and possible future trends

Our response to the demographic challenge should include a rise in the age of retirement. Healthy ageing for many people makes this possible and an increase in employment rates among older people is now occurring.

## the UK pensions system: position and trends

The UK pensions system appeared in the past to work well because one of the least generous state pension systems in the developed world was complemented by the most developed system of voluntary private funded pension. This rosy picture always hid multiple inadequacies relating to specific groups of people, but on average the system worked, with the percentage of GDP transferred to pensioners comparable to other countries. But the state plans to provide decreasing support for many people in order to control expenditure in the face of an ageing population and the private system is not developing to offset the state's retreat role. Instead it is in significant decline. . . .

The underlying level of funded pension saving is falling rather than rising to meet the demographic challenge, pension right accrual is becoming still more unequal, and risk is being shifted to individuals sometimes ill-equipped to deal with it.

## looking forward: pension adequacy if trends unchanged

Given present trends many people will face 'inadequate' pensions in retirement, unless they have large non-pension assets or are intending to retire much later than current retirees.

## non-pension savings and housing

. . . But the ownership of [non-pension financial] assets is very unequally distributed and for the majority of people they can only provide a modest contribution to their standard of living in retirement. . . .

But house ownership does not provide a sufficient solution to the problem of pension provision given (i) the uncertainty over future house prices; (ii) other potential claims on housing wealth such as long-term care; and (iii) the fact that housing wealth is not significantly higher among those with least pension rights.

## barriers to a voluntarist solution

The present level of pension right accrual, private and state combined, will leave many with inadequate pensions. And there are likely to be limits to solving the problem solely via increased retirement ages. If state system plans are taken as given, a higher level of private saving is required.

Unless new government initiatives can make a major difference to behaviours it is unlikely that the present voluntary private system combined with the present state system will solve the problem of inadequate pension savings.

## revitalised voluntarism, changes to the state system or increased compulsion?

To achieve adequacy there are three possible ways forward:

(i)    a major revitalisation of the voluntary system; and/or

(ii)   significant changes to the state system; and/or

(iii)  an increased level of compulsory private pension saving beyond that already implicit within the UK system.

## women and pensions

Women pensioners in the UK today are significantly poorer than men. This reflects both labour market features (lower employment rates, lower average earnings, and more part-time work) and specific features of the UK's state pension system. These state system features have in the past entailed most women gaining pension income through their husband, and reflected assumptions about family structure which have ceased to be valid. An effective pension system for the future must be one in which the vast majority of women accrue pension entitlements, both state and private, in their own right.

# further reading and resources

The resources break down into four broad categories:

1 books;
2 newspapers and journals;
3 leaflets and similar publications;
4 websites.

There may be a degree of overlap in that some newspaper articles and leaflets may also be available on the publisher's website.

I divide my suggestions into general and specific. General relates to the subject as a whole whereas specific denotes particular chapters. They are by no means exhaustive but will hopefully provide a start.

## general suggestions

### books

Major bookshops stock a range of books on personal finance. As to textbooks to take the subject further, you may like to consider:

- Callaghan, G., Fribbance I. and Higginson, M. (eds): *Personal Finance* (Hoboken, NJ: Wiley, 2006)
- Harrison, D. *Personal Financial Planning: Theory and Practice* (Harlow: FT, Prentice Hall, 2005)

The Consumers' Association (www.which.co.uk) publishes a range of books on personal finance and related subjects. Details appear on its website (see below).

Several chapters involve legal topics and the following book covers welfare benefits and tax credits, insolvency, wills (but not trusts), pensions, housing and the consumer:

- Pritchard, J. The New Penguin Guide to the Law (London: Penguin Books, 2004)

## newspapers and journals

Some of the weekend newspapers carry supplements with coverage of personal finance. In particular, the Saturday/Sunday *FT* has a section called "FT Money" that is directed to personal finance and investment. As well as articles on topical subjects, it includes a "Databank" divided into "Savings and Investments", "Debt" and "Companies and Markets" that draws together statistical information of interest to private investors (including deposit and lending rates). The "FT Companies & Markets" section of the newspaper reports on business and company news, share prices and managed fund prices.

The monthly magazine of the Consumers' Association *Which?* includes reports on matters of personal finance. You may find copies in your local library.

Magazines published monthly include:

- *Money Management* (aimed especially at independent advisers)
- *Money Observer*
- *Money Wise*

## leaflets and similar publications

The Community Legal Service publishes a series of booklets in the CLS Direct Information Leaflet series that may be found in your local library. The bookets are also available online at www.clsdirect.org.uk.

## websites

The Financial Services Authority has a comprehensive website for consumers (www.moneymadeclear.fsa.gov.uk). I quote from "Consumer Publications":
Use the site to:

- shop around with our comparative tables – including mortgages, pensions and ISAs;
- check a firm is authorised by the FSA, or is the agent of an authorised firm. If they are not authorised you will not have access to complaints and compensation schemes if things go wrong;
- order any of our wide range of consumer publications;
- report any misleading financial advertising;
- see explanations of financial products in plain English;
- read news articles about firms and products.

BBC2 Working Lunch www.bbc.co.uk/workinglunch (includes a broadband-player facility to view programmes).

The Consumers' Association (www.which.co.uk).

Moneyfacts describes itself (www.moneyfacts.co.uk) as "the independent and unbiased website helping you to make informed decisions on personal finances with independent and unbiased financial comparison". It covers a wide range of personal financial services with sections on "Best Buys" and "Learn about . . .".

The *FT* website (www.ft.com).

## suggestions for specific chapters

### chapter 3  the basic tools

The Consumer Credit Counselling Service website (www.cccs.co.uk) has some excellent material on preparing a budget through its "Budget Advice" link.

For claiming state benefits, a good starting point is the DWP website (www.dwp.gov.uk) with links to:

- Child Support Agency (www.csa.gov.uk)
- Disability and Carers' Service (www.dwp.gov.uk/dcs)
- Jobcentre Plus (www.jobcentreplus.gov.uk)
- The Pension Service (www.thepensionservice.gov.uk).

The HMRC website is www.hmrc.gov.uk.

Two of the CLS Direct Information Leaflets are helpful:

- 9 'Welfare Benefits (Your legal rights)'
- 19 'Community Care'.

### chapter 5  borrowing

Magazines that specialise on mortgages include *What Mortgage* (monthly).

A number of websites provide information on the theory and practice of borrowing and what to do if in difficulty. Here is a selection:

- Citizens Advice (www.citizensadvice.org.uk/cabdir.ihtml)
- Community Legal Service (www.clsdirect.org.uk)
- Consumer Credit Counselling Service (www.cccs.co.uk)
- Council of Mortgage Lenders (www.cml.org.uk)
- Financial Services Authority (www.moneymadeclear.fsa.org.uk)
- National Debtline (www.nationaldebtline.co.uk)
- Office of Fair Trading (www.oft.gov.uk).

Credit reference agencies:

- Call Credit (www.callcredit.co.uk)

- Equifax (www.equifax.co.uk)
- Experian (www.experian.co.uk).

There is also the CLS Direct Information Leaflet 1, "Dealing with Debt (Your Legal Rights)".

## chapter 6  insurance and assurance

Websites that provide information include:

- Association of British Insurers (www.abi.org.uk)
- Moneyfacts (www.moneyfacts.co.uk)
- Insurance companies' websites (geared to their own products).

## chapter 7  taxation

A reasonably comprehensive book that covers all the major taxes is:

- Foreman, A. and G. Mowles *Zurich Tax Handbook 2006–07* (Harlow: Pearson Education, 2006)

In a lighter vein, two books produced anually are:

- Gender, D. B. *Daily Telegraph Tax Guide* (Macmillan)
- Vass, J. *Daily Mail Tax Guide* (Profile Books).

Her Majesty's Revenue and Customs website (www.hmrc.gov.uk) gives access to a wide range of leaflets and other guidance.

## chapter 8  making your money work and chapter 9  investment: an art or a science?

You may wish to consider the following books for further reading:

- Arnold, G. *Financial Times Guide to Investing: The Definitive Companion to Investment and the Financial Markets* (London: FT Prentice Hall, 2004)
- Cahill, M. *An Investor's Guide to Analyzing Companies & Valuing Shares: How to Make the Right Investment Decision* (London: FT Prentice Hall, 2003)
- Graham, B. *The Intelligent Investor* (revised edition) (New York: HarperBusiness Essentials, c. 2003)
- Gray, B. *Investors Chronicle Beginners Guide to Investment* (Sydney: Century; London: Business Books, 1993)
- Leach, R. *The Investor's Guide to Understanding Accounts* (Petersfield: Harriman House, 2004)
- Train, J. *The Midas Touch: The Strategies that Have Made Warren Buffett America's Pre-eminent Investor* (Petersfield: Harriman House Classics, 2003)
- Vaitilingam, R. *The Financial Times Guide to Using the Financial Pages* (Harlow: FT Prentice Hall, 2006).

Magazines include:

- *Investors Chronicle* (weekly, focus is on quoted companies with some coverage of other forms of investment)
- *What Investment* (monthly, aimed at private investors, broad content including collectives)

Websites:

- *Financial Times* (www.ft.com
- *Investors Chronicle* (www.investorschronicle.co.uk)
- Trustnet (comprehensive statistics on collectives) (www.trustnet.com)
- Investment Management Association (for information on unit trusts and OEICs) (www.investmentuk.org)
- Association of Investment Companies (for information on investment trusts) (www.theaic.co.uk)
- Moneyfacts (www.moneyfacts.co.uk)
- Quoted companies' and fund management companies' own sites

## chapter 10  wills and trusts

You may wish to consider two books from the Consumers' Association:

- *Wills and Probate*
- *The Which? Guide to Giving and Inheriting* (includes two chapters on trusts)

The Society of Trust and Estate Practitioners publishes leaflets:

- "Why Make a Trust?"
- "Why Make a Will?"

that can be downloaded from www.step.org

## chapter 11  pensions

Books that are reasonably digestible include:

- Ward, S. *Your Guide to Pensions 2006: Planning Ahead to Boost Retirement Income* (London: Age Concern England, 2005)
- Consumers' Association: *The Pension Handbook*

Websites:

- The Pensions Service (re the state schemes) (www.thepensionservice.gov.uk)
- The Pensions Advisory Service (www.pensionsadvisoryservice.org.uk).

## chapter 12  buying a home

CLS Direct Information Leaflet 5, 'Buying and Selling Property'

Commercial websites to find property include:

- www.primemove.com
- www.propertyfinder.com
- www.rightmove.co.uk)

## chapter 13  growing old gracefully

Range of books published by Age Concern (www.ageconcern.org.uk/bookshop).

Book published by the Consumers' Association:

- *The Which? Guide to Giving and Inheriting*

Age Concern Factsheet 10:

- 'Local Authority Charging Procedures for Care Homes'

CLS Direct Information Leaflets:

- 9 Welfare Benefits (Your Legal Rights)
- 19 Community Care (Your Legal Rights)
- 28 Dealing with Someone Else's Affairs

Websites:

- Age Concern (www.ageconcern.org.uk)
- Alzheimer's Society (www.alzheimers.org.uk)
- Commission for Social Care Inspection (www.csci.org.uk)
- Department of Health (www.dh.gov.uk)
- Disability and Carers' Service (www.dwp.gov.uk/dcs)
- Financial Services Authority (www.moneymadeclear.fsa.org.uk)
- Help the Aged (www.helptheaged.org.uk)
- Her Majesty's Revenue and Customs (www.hmrc.gov.uk)
- Local authorities' sites
- Pension Service (www.thepensionservice.gov.uk)
- Public Guardianship Office (www.guardianship.gov.uk)
- Safe Home Income Plans (SHIP) (www.ship-ltd.org).

## chapter 15  looking after your interests

'Advisers Investigated': a survey on financial advisers, *Which?* Sept. 2006, pp. 20–3:

Websites (to find advisers and for other information):

- Association of British Insurers (www.abi.org.uk)
- Association of Private Client Investment Managers (represents investment managers and stockbrokers) (www.apcims.co.uk)
- Chartered Institute of Taxation and Association of Tax Technicians (www.tax.org)
- Council of Mortgage Lenders (www.cml.org.uk)
- Institute of Chartered Accountants in England and Wales (www.icaew.co.uk)
- Institute of Financial Planning (www.financialplanning.org.uk)
- Law Society (www.lawsoc.org.uk)
- Society of Financial Advisers (www.sofa.org)
- Society of Trust and Estate Practitioners (www.step.org).

Websites (regulatory organisations):

- Financial Services Authority (www.moneymadeclear.fsa.org.uk)
- Financial Services Ombudsman (www.financial-ombudsman.org.uk)
- Office of Fair Trading (www.oft.gov.uk)
- Pensions Ombudsman (www.pensions-ombudsman.org.uk).

index